Any Girl
Mia Döring

**A Memoir of
Sexual Exploitation
and Recovery**

HACHETTE
BOOKS
IRELAND

First published in Ireland in 2022 by HACHETTE BOOKS IRELAND

1

Cataloguing in Publication Data is available from the British Library

ISBN 978 1 52937 181 9

Typeset in Garamond Premier Pro by Bookends Publishing Services, Dublin.
Printed and bound in Great Britain by Clays Ltd, Elcograf S.p.A.

Hachette Books Ireland policy is to use papers that are natural, renewable and
recyclable products and made from wood grown in sustainable forests. The logging
and manufacturing processes are expected to conform to the environmental
regulations of the country of origin.

Hachette Books Ireland
8 Castlecourt Centre
Castleknock
Dublin 15, Ireland

A division of Hachette UK Ltd
Carmelite House, 50 Victoria Embankment, London EC4Y 0DZ

www.hachettebooksireland.ie

Any Girl

Mia Döring is a writer and psychotherapist specialising in sexual trauma. She lives and works in Dublin. Her essays, fiction and articles have been published in *Litro Magazine*, *The Bohemyth*, *Ropes Journal* and *Huffington Post*. *Any Girl* is her first book.

CONTENTS

Opening My Eyes Underwater 3

The Last One 11

The Places that Scare You 19

People-Pleaser 47

Love and Death 75

Stupid Girl 89

Possum 99

Comfort Women 115

Berlin 145

Rape, or the Beginning 163

Trauma 199

Love and Men 229

My Body 263

Surrendering 291

Acknowledgements 308

Further Reading 313

For the truth tellers

The conflict between the will to deny horrible events and the will to proclaim them aloud is the central dialectic of psychological trauma.

Judith Lewis Herman, *Trauma and Recovery: The Aftermath of Violence – From Domestic Abuse to Political Terror*

… tell as much of the truth as one can bear, and then tell a little more.

James Baldwin, *The Cross of Redemption: Uncollected Writings*

OPENING MY EYES UNDERWATER

The first time I opened my eyes underwater, I was seven. My swimming teacher was this tall, sinewy, Aertex-wearing woman with a 'boy haircut', called Linda. She was tough, serious and terrifying. She didn't acquiesce to welling-up eyes or whining or trembling lips or anything else we did to avoid the scary things she sometimes made us do, like opening our eyes underwater. I don't know what I was afraid of. The unknown below, I suppose.

Linda had a thing. She made us dip our heads beneath the surface and would stick a hand in front of our faces. When we surfaced, we had to tell her how many fingers she'd been holding out, so you couldn't fake it. I would hover at the side of the pool, gripping the bar, feigning illness, jealously looking on at the others dipping up and down. When I tried to do it, I couldn't open my squeezed-shut eyes. I'd psych myself up, go under and freeze. I could feel the sting of the chlorinated water trying to get through my tightly shut eyelids. I'd pop back up and shake my head at Linda, defeated.

3

Then one day I must have got tired of hovering or maybe I could no longer take Linda's brand of encouragement – shouting – and I opened my eyes. The water stung, like I knew it would, but my prize was there: a blurry fist with a blurry thumb sticking out. I'd done it.

I popped back up. 'One!' I shouted. Linda winked at me and moved on to the next child. I floated backwards, weightless. I had been courageous. I had opened my eyes underwater and now the possibilities were endless. My capabilities were expanding. I felt high on my very own self.

In the past eight years, I have written anonymously about a hidden part of my life. I have supplied testimonies, reflections, stories and articles, parts of a theatre production, and speeches. I have collaborated with extraordinary people and organisations working to end the ever-rising epidemic of male violence against women. I've had the privilege of delivering testimony and expertise to NGOs and charities, politicians, journalists and students. I worked on a domestic-abuse helpline. I delivered a TEDx talk on rape. I have connected with sexual-violence survivors and activists all over the world. President Michael D. Higgins wrote to me about a speech I had given asking for male involvement in combating sexual violence. His letter is framed underneath a photo of us at Áras an Uachtaráin. Sometimes I read it over and over because his words, 'Your message is one of radical truth', make me remember that my words actually matter.

I have also watched Dáil Éireann debates and Seanad Éireann hearings from the public gallery, listening to my trauma being debated and wilfully misrepresented. There were times when I had to leave the gallery and gulp in air, unable to listen any longer.

I became a psychotherapist and have experienced the joy and profound privilege of connecting with people in a way that can be rare for us in our everyday lives. I have connected with sex-trade survivors from all over the world, working on ending prostitution internationally. Unfortunately, none of this has been enough to bury my own truth, which has been rising dangerously inside me.

Much of the activism was like a version of me hanging around the swimming pool of my childhood, afraid to open my eyes. The anonymous work frustrated me and limited me, practically and psychologically. My unreadiness and perceived cowardice frustrated me. My innumerable fears stunted me. I thought if I poured all my passion for ending male violence towards women into working against rape and sexual abuse, into helping to heal the aftermath, it would squash the urge to tell my stories.

But, in the work I did, I always felt like I was half of myself, still holding back, never able to really fill out to my own borders, afraid of being fully seen.

People would say to me that I was brave to tell the one story I was okay with telling, and I would shiver away from their words, feeling like a lying coward. I wasn't ready, and I'm still not, but here I am: sometimes we need to stop testing the water and just stick our heads under and open our eyes.

We always know when the time is right.

The timing will never be right.

It will never be as bad as we think.

Summer 2018

I bring my dog to the beach. It takes about five minutes to get there. When we reach the steps from the railway bridge, I let her off the lead and she runs to the sand, ears back, her small, white body an arrow. She weaves her way through the waves, ankle-deep in the gentle surf. She stops and looks back to make sure I'm following.

When the tide is out, we go to the far end where it's quieter, sliding over seaweed. I stare at the sea. I like the slate-grey days when the sea and the sky meld into one entity. In the summer, in sunny weather, the beach is full of people. Its energy shifts and it becomes a new place, not ours. The dog and I self-consciously pick our way around parents, children and rubbish, and I feel displaced, outside things.

On warm days like today, I sit on the walkway, absorbing the heat of the stone underneath me while the dog sniffs around. This place is as close to a sanctuary as I've ever experienced. The water is nearby, rippling in and out of pockets of rocks and boulders. Today it is grey-green, my favourite colour for the sea to be. It tries to pull you in. Every day is different in this place. The water is a balm, forming and re-forming. Passers-by grin at us. I like it when people say something to me about the dog. I feel like a normal person for two minutes. I like it when people talk to me full stop. I take out my phone and text my best friend about minding my god-daughter at the weekend.

I am a person watching her dog dig holes in the sand. I am a person looking at the turnstones running in packs over the seaweed. I am a person looking past the Martello tower to the Poolbeg chimneys, over to Howth, the boats, the kids doing their sailing courses, the back of the west pier. I join the dog on the sand and we scuff about. If I see a good stone, I put it into my pocket. I could stay here all day, but the dog is harassing a trio of small children, and the parents are looking over at me pointedly.

At home, I spot the enormous pile of newsprint stacked in my hallway. A friend is running for the local elections and has asked me to deliver the Social Democrats' paper in my locality. I'd reluctantly agreed. 'Listen to podcasts,' she'd said, dropping six hundred copies in my hallway.

I go out with a hundred of them. As I deliver them, I do not listen to podcasts.

I think, I think, I think.

I walk from house to house and I think.

Do I write this or not? Is there any other way? Do I have to break my parents' hearts? Do I have to hurt the people I love? Do I have to sacrifice so much? Do I have to jeopardise my psychotherapy practice? What will happen to me? Will anything I write in the future be taken seriously? Will I ever be loved again? Will I only ever be known for the contents of this book?

An irate yellow-haired woman shouts at me for delivering 'junk mail' to her house and, absurdly, tears well in my eyes. Also absurdly, I remind myself that I am a good person.

At home, I eye my laptop lying on the kitchen table. I make a coffee and sit down at it.

I live from day to day, moment to moment, breath to breath. Life becomes microscopic when a big thing is coming. Until this book is done, my life, my future, is on pause, and I am in limbo. I suppose I am trying to liberate myself.

Trauma holds on to us and keeps us clinging to the rail until we are ready to let go. I see everything through a lens located in the past.

I have to live my life.

The only way I know of doing that is to write it all down.

This is me declaring myself.

It's going to change everything.

It's going to be okay.

That is the mystery about writing: it comes
out of afflictions, out of the gouged times,
when the heart is cut open.

Edna O'Brien, *Country Girl*

THE LAST ONE

The last punter is in his mid-thirties, you guess. You are twenty-four years old, and you arrive at the apartment block in South County Dublin, tucked behind a street of enormous houses and lines of large, leafy trees. You are there to do a job and get home again. It's about 9 p.m. You ring the buzzer. You're not feeling anything in particular as you wait to be let in. He has asked you for thirty minutes of your time.

When you get to his apartment, the door is already slightly ajar, so you slide in, saying, 'Hello?' into the dark. He is tall, standing with his back to you in the middle of an enormous living room, his hands on his hips. He's watching muted American football on a gigantic flat-screen television. The floor is strewn with crisp wrappers, empty takeaway boxes and clothes.

He turns his head, as if he has forgotten he buzzed you into the building. He doesn't say hello or make any small-talk and you're a little thrown. Most men say something to ease the awkwardness they're feeling. Usually your role is to make the man feel comfortable, and you're really good at that.

This man is completely comfortable in the situation. He

walks backwards towards you, eyes glued to the screen and cash in his hands, which he passes to you.

'Have you got change?' he says.

'No, sorry,' you say, and he makes a face, annoyed.

'Is there somewhere I can get changed?' you ask, and he directs you to the bathroom where the bath is used as a storage space for magazines and books. The unwashed sink is lined with scum and covered in congealed toothpaste and the mat on the floor is grey with dirt. You wedge yourself behind the door to avoid having to go too far in, and carefully take off most of your clothes.

There is a thing you do now before going back in. You put on a mask of sorts, like going out on stage to play a character. You will be what the script calls you to be, and the actual you, whoever that is, is tucked away inside, unseen. You take a breath.

The punter is standing where you left him, watching the television, hands still absurdly on hips. You give him your biggest smile, to dredge some human connection from him. You need to elicit a smile.

He does not smile. He barely notices that you're back. He unbuckles his belt in preparation for a blowjob. Ten years later, you will still hate the sound or the sight of a belt unbuckling, but, in that moment, you are not yet aware of what you are doing to yourself.

His penis tastes like sour milk and smells like it hasn't

been washed in days. You ask him to put on a condom, and he does so, almost as if he was expecting it. The rubbery taste of condom doesn't conceal the smell, but you try your best to get it over with by working quickly and feigning enthusiasm.

He holds your hair in one hand and aggressively pushes and pulls your head back and forth. You are used to it (you can get used to anything). You glance up and he is still watching the television, rubbing his stomach with his other hand. You experience the feeling that comes from total objectification, your humanity erased. To him, you are non-human; you do not exist. You close your eyes and concentrate on breathing. You can feel your eyes watering.

'You're so beautiful,' he mutters. 'Oh, my God, you're so beautiful sucking my dick. You're so beautiful choking on my cock.' He repeats this over and over, still staring at the screen, still rubbing his stomach. You can't catch a breath. He doesn't think you're beautiful. He isn't even looking at you. He doesn't know what beauty is.

Every shove of his dick into the back of your throat proves you're worthless, that you're just a whore, you don't deserve tenderness, that this is where your value lies. If you are not a whore, then what are you doing on the floor in front of this man, feigning enthusiasm for getting face-fucked? There is no façade here, as there is with most of them, who smile as they keep up a pretence of this being somehow acceptable.

He starts to smack the side of your face lightly and you feel on edge. You possess the wordless knowledge that when a man doesn't see you as a human being, he can do anything to you. He smacks you a little harder, forcing you to kneel up and steady yourself to keep your balance. He pulls your head back and smacks you so hard across the face that you fall to the side. All your breath comes right up your throat and your whole body flushes with heat. You are stunned.

The left side of your face is hot and tingling with pain, and you go to touch it, but he is on you already, pushing you down on your stomach, grabbing your hair as he attempts to have anal sex with you. You struggle away from him, and he says casually, puzzled, 'Do you not do anal?'

He's gripping your hair and neck and you can feel all your muscles tightening. It's hard to say no when you've been paid; in order to form the words, you'd have to believe it was an option open to you.

To punters, that is what women in the sex trade are for: to do with what they want you to do, for a price. To have power over a woman. To have sex when and where and how they want. That is the point. That is the kick of it. By resisting, you are going against this agreement. Of course, the man is wrong to try to force anal sex on you, but you can't say so because you don't know what will happen if you do. It could get worse. You are alone in an apartment with a much stronger, much bigger person. It is easier, psychologically, to get through it quietly and persuade yourself that what is happening is fine, rather than to put yourself in more danger.

You will remember the sensation of his rough fingers against your face for more than a decade. You will recall this sensation vividly and say a prayer to a God you're not sure you believe in that one day it might fade. Then he takes your hair in his fist again and pulls it back so far that you can't breathe. You think he might pull it out. You think you're going to die. But then he releases you and lets your face drop back to the floor.

He shoves himself into your vagina without warning. He is rough and it hurts, but all you feel is relief. You're practically grateful to him. You fawn, want to please him. It takes him only a few minutes to finish. You look at the carpet, disappear into its dark blueness, then at the freckle on your right wrist, there for as long as you can remember.

You leave through wrought-iron gates. The dark tarmac is like liquid underfoot. The sky above is black, the air cold against your face. You sit in the car and it hurts to breathe. Your body and bones ache. Your neck is sore and other places are numb. You feel the soft car seat beneath you. You reverse out of the car space just like you do on any other day.

How did you end up here? Why are you doing this? It

seems to have happened like a natural disaster, rather than in any steps you can recognise. But even natural disasters have methodology, though they might seem like spontaneous chaos from the outside.

You drive back into the city centre, into your normal everyday life. Your housemates, your friends, your art.

This is where it ends. This suburb is where you're going to leave it. In the end, all it took was one hard slap across your face.

Only to the extent that we expose ourselves over and over to annihilation can that which is indestructible be found in us.

Pema Chödrön, *When Things Fall Apart*

THE PLACES THAT SCARE YOU

I don't remember how it happened.

A psychotherapist who had worked with men who paid for sex told me they seemed to 'find themselves in it'. The same way I found myself in it. I don't understand how you can make decisions like that and not be aware of it, but it happened to me.

I work with women in their early twenties and I look at their faces, their careful mannerisms, their insecurities, the curated confidence veiling fragile vulnerabilities. They question every aspect of their behaviour. They feel chronically not good enough. They don't value themselves or what they bring to the lives of others. They doubt themselves, their friendships. They are hard on themselves. They struggle to know who they are and how to be in the world. Their biggest fear is judgement.

I know many men in their forties. I wonder if they are capable of letting a twenty-one-year-old student go down on them for fifty quid, knowing what it means to be that age. Would they lie to themselves and tell themselves it's acceptable? Are the men who deny they would allow this to happen just good actors?

By the time I was twenty-one, my body was a device: using it for money was no problem and getting paid for sexual acts felt *pretty good*. It gave me a sense of control and power, the things I needed to re-own my stolen body. I had nothing to lose. I could pay the bills, buy nicer food. I deserved it! My body was mine, not anyone else's. I could do what I wanted with it.

This is the bit I don't remember. It was the days before most people had the internet at home, before social media and smartphones, before even having your own laptop, so I have no idea how I researched this, or thought or felt about it. The option of escorting seemed to take solid shape without my having considered it in depth.

I don't remember doing it, but I know I used an ad online, and I did it. It just happened. I found myself there, just like that therapist said.

When I was small, I wanted to be a marine biologist when I grew up. Then I could be near whales, dolphins and sharks all the time and be in and around the deep sea. I appreciate its danger and mystery. When I'm walking the dog on the beach and the tide is out, I look down and remind myself that I'm walking on the seabed. The profundity of it stops me in my tracks. I get up on the black rocks that are usually immersed and unseen and feel a wordless awe for how something can be one thing and then a few hours later be something else, no longer deep or dangerous. I do not know why I find this so awe-inspiring. I am always blown away by the sea. I swim in it and understand its power, the tow, the pull, the depth. When I was swimming as a child, I always found the cloudy water of the Irish Sea much more exciting than the crystal clear water of foreign countries, where you could see everything and everything could see you.

As an escort, I liked having a secret part of my life. I didn't feel any shame, perhaps because nobody knew what I was doing. I decided whom I saw and how much they paid. Those men would pay to access my body. That was how much they thought of me. That was how valuable I was. They thought I was *beautiful* and they wanted me. I needed to feel beautiful and wanted. What was I without this sexual validation? Just a teenager who had got into a weird situation with an older man.

'What's a girl like you doing this for?'

I didn't like that question, laughed it off. It pointed too closely to a truth. There was no girl like me. There was just whoever I was to whichever man.

To avoid the uncomfortable feelings of disappointment, emptiness and sadness, I let myself be absorbed into the other person so that I could erase myself and my own feelings. If I could understand who they were and what they needed, I could focus on them, and not notice how *I* felt. If we take responsibility for someone else's emotional state, we can avoid being responsible for our own.

I always found a way to relate to these men. I am intuitive, instinctively able to mirror and accommodate various personalities. The bigger the personality, the more I would shrink to allow him more space. My warmth and communication skills put these men at ease, made them comfortable. My sheer friendliness sometimes disarmed them. I encountered the full spectrum of humanity: entitlement, humour, bullying, intimidation, generosity, violence – all of it. It encountered me.

I don't remember the first one. For some reason, I can't remember any of it and it sometimes frustrates me not to have ownership over this significant memory. I've tried to remember, but there is only a void. It bothers me and doesn't bother me. Sometimes I feel a sense of gratitude that the memory is beyond my grasp.

There are fractured memories of lifts, stairs, hotel reception desks, faces, wide suburban roads, the tops of buses, car parks, all displaced and surreal. The worst memories used to hit me from nowhere and sometimes they still do. I feel an inner floating when these memories come in, as if I have escaped the visceral part of it, whooshed out from inside myself. I become very still and stay quiet while the ripping apart takes place beneath my skin.

A few years ago after a Christmas market in Smithfield, my friends and I said goodbye around the corner from where I had parked. In my rush to meet them, I didn't realise I had parked right in front of the glass doors to an apartment block I had been into years earlier, where I was handed two hundred euro and huge objects were put inside me. The abuse was framed as a game, as some sort of sexual exploration for the small man who had hired me. I didn't know until I arrived that the apartment was owned by a couple who rented their spare bedroom to punters.

As I was leaving, they were sitting in the kitchen, consulting with the small man in hushed tones. He tried to broker a deal with them, a deal for my body. The idea was that I would work for them and be rented to punters in their sex room. I declined the offer, despite the best efforts of the small man, who seemed to be trying to act as my pimp.

As I hugged my friends goodbye, I saw the glass doors. The images were there, and I was now separate to my friends. They were normal, good people, their lives and bodies untainted. I was filthy and should not have brought my disgusting body into their lives. How hilarious that I had tried to be normal. How pathetic of me to forget for a moment what I was.

One man calls you and picks you up from wherever you are in the city or at college and brings you somewhere – his home, a hotel room – and all he wants is to feel your boobs and get a blowjob and it's always over within a few minutes. It's the easiest job because he's kind and doesn't want to have sex with you. Shaved chin and beer belly. Shiny black hair. He tells you about brothel raids he's heard about, and you feel jealous that he goes to anyone but you: you're about twenty-one and he's about forty-five, and you want to feel special. He's a carpenter and works all over the city centre, so he calls you quite often.

You go the whole way out to Swords to see a chirpy guy in his thirties who blabbers on about his girlfriend being away for the weekend with her friends, how she knows about his 'addiction to prostitutes' but thinks it's all over with now. She took him back, trusted him again. Tall and fit with stubble on his face and glinting, mischievous eyes. You perch on the side of the bed, and here he is telling you all about it, dick in hand. He's yapping as if he's discussing the weather or his plans for the weekend. He says he's more careful now. He sees escorts only on his lunch break or when his girlfriend is away, like now. He's really funny, and you like him despite his apparent lack of any conscience.

The ability of the men to lie to their partners is amazing. It's not like it's an affair, with feelings, they say. They know what they have is precious; they just don't respect it. This thing they do is so woven into their lives that lying has become natural. Telling their wives that they'll be home at eight instead of seven. So easy to say again and again. You don't really care: it's none of your business. He fucks you hard in the spare room, so fast you can't breathe, and you go home with 250 euro.

You are regularly visited by this young guy in his late twenties who gives out about his girlfriend the entire time. He is short and weedy, and wears hoodies and runners. He talks non-stop and it's draining because part of the job is to be present to the punter. He's too interested. He asks questions. 'Why are you doing this? Most of the girls are foreign. What got you into it?'

He looks around the room and picks up things you have left out, puts them down again. You feel exposed and you're annoyed with him. But why should it matter that he's holding one of your cheap bracelets, turning it over in his hands? Why should that have any impact on you whatsoever?

You go to an empty apartment where an electrician wants a call-out on his lunch break, and he fucks you beside the mirrored wardrobe, so you're confronted with yourself the whole time. You can't remember anything about him.

A man in his early fifties rents you for an hour. Tall, skinny, big long nose, reddish face, tiny eyes. He wears a shirt and a tie. He sits on the side of the bed and the three fifty-euro notes slide out of his hands onto the floor. You don't know if it was an accident or not. You both look at them. He smiles expectantly, waiting for you to pick up your money, which you do. Then he lies back and unbuckles his belt in preparation for a blowjob, and the humiliation in that moment is complete.

You visit men in hotel rooms all over Dublin. You are cheerful and caring. 'A breath of fresh air,' says one fifty-year-old man. 'So obedient,' says another, and your stomach shrinks. Most of them are middle-aged, middle-class, married and wealthy. They live in nice houses, have big cars and fat wallets with pictures of their families. Seeing you is a hobby they feel entitled to indulge. They express no emotion. They like to try new girls. They say they want to 'try' you, and you feel grateful that you've been selected. You actually feel special that they picked you. And you feel special that you are able to sell sex – that you have the guts and confidence to do it.

You deal with the men through your disarming openness and friendliness, never showing or experiencing any feeling. You accept them exactly as they are. *You* are in charge and *you* are empowered – *This is what we've been told to do, isn't it? If sex sells, why shouldn't I profit? The men are the idiots: they're paying for something as easy to give as sex.*

You go out to the suburbs, to a flat above a pizza shop. The young man who answers the door is tall, slight and somewhat intellectually disabled. You didn't know it before you met him and now you're here you can't leave, and you want to make him happy even more than you do the others. You have to mind him. It feels wrong. You tell yourself, *This will be over in twenty minutes.*

The memories are patchy. His face and the closeness of his body to yours. The pointy parts of his body jabbing into your soft parts. The way he pushes you backwards. He kisses you with open watery eyes, his face mashed against yours. You soothe him, always soothing. You have to be present to him to make sure he's safe. The tension you felt when the door opened has curled itself into a hard ball in your stomach. It stays tight and unmoving until you close the door behind you on your way out. There is no façade here, and it is heartbreaking in its starkness. Afterwards, you cry in the car.

When a man calls, you have to weigh up what he might be like, if there is anything off about him. His tone of voice, accent, age group, what he says and how he says it, all create a vague picture of someone being okay or not. Because you aren't very considerate of your wellbeing, you usually give someone the benefit of the doubt, unless they're blatantly abusive on the phone. You mostly ignore the niggle in the base of your stomach, or see it as a test. The goal you have set yourself is that you can make any man happy so, if you can't, you have failed.

Men call you and keep you on the phone for as long as possible. They detail what they want to do to you as they have a wank. Some men call persistently until you have to block them. They send text messages that say, 'Are you working now?' Or, more usually, 'Where are you based?'

You're kind and funny and generous, so generous (you give it all away), and you know how to make them feel good, which makes you feel good. You like feeling like a thing. You like playing roles, being a vacant container into which the punter delivers his expectations of how you should be, and you fulfil them. Not having to know yourself is a relief. Part of you wants it because you know how it works. Part of you wants it because you feel you don't deserve to be treated gently.

You see a man in his sixties in his city-centre apartment. He has rented you as a birthday present to himself. It doesn't occur to you that it's weird a man forty years older than you wants to have sex with you. He's a big, tall, straight-up man with lots of white hair. He wears a waistcoat. He pays you five hundred euro for two hours of your time, and you like him a lot. He is respectful and gentle. You expected it might be hard because, earlier in the day, he'd sent you a text message specifying how you should have your hair tied up, but it turns out that he is kind and doesn't even penetrate you. You never even see his penis and feel grateful, but you cannot yet reflect on why that might be.

When you are young, you don't know where the danger is or the harm is. You learn by doing. As you get older, you recognise things more quickly. You learn that older people are not necessarily wise or to be trusted.

You open the door to see the man waiting for you on the bed. Short, early fifties. Dark, dark hair and black eyes. He is looking up at you with his big, dead eyes and you feel that something is off. He doesn't speak or smile or make any sort of gesture to communicate, bar the unrelenting eye contact. His gaze is ice cold, as if he could comfortably kill you. He is like a wall. Threat is in the air: it rushes up your chest and claws at your throat. You've only been doing this for a couple of months and you don't know how to respond to him. He remains silent, unbuckles his belt for a blowjob and presents you with a type of penis you have never seen in your short life. It looks as if there is something wrong with it. You know it isn't normal. It is disgusting. You don't know what to do. But maybe it is normal, and it would be rude to point it out. He is a grown man – he must know about these things.

You force yourself to give him a blowjob because he's paying you and that's what you said you'd do and you're only twenty-one and he's more than twice your age. You feel him on your lips and in your mouth. You smell his smell. But you are polite and you are scared and you are getting paid to do this.

Fourteen years later, the image of him staring at you and the corresponding physical sensations will still materialise. Your body will not let you forget it.

You go to college and make your art and see your friends, and everything is normal. The escorting exists in a separate bubble. You do it whenever you need some extra money. You like scheduling your 'clients'. It feels grown-up to have these secret plans. You like getting the cash. It feels powerful and important to be handed a hundred and fifty euro. It feels important to keep an eye on the time, to make sure you don't run over the thirty minutes that the one hundred and fifty euro pays for. It feels grown-up to throw the cash into a drawer, where very often you forget about it. You tell yourself you 'need the money', but looking at it makes you feel uneasy, and you spend it quickly, sometimes on paying bills, more often on insignificant, superficial things like make-up, just to get rid of it. The money is both coercive and compensatory. It cleans it up, makes it okay, gives you a small thrill.

One time, you spend the money on a Christmas gift for someone, and a college friend asks how you could afford it. You say you'd saved for it and the words feel sticky, like tar, in your mouth.

I must be a dark, terrible person, you think, *to be able to lie so easily about this*. Lie about where you got money and lie about where you were going and lie about where you have been. *I must have an extraordinary darkness inside me.*

Sometimes, especially in the United States, the sex trade is referred to as 'the life', because of how all-consuming it is. It has a way of wrapping its vines around your throat, keeping you locked in, and making that feel like the safest and easiest place to be.

You take the bus out to a northside suburb to see a punter, and get lost trying to find your way around the wide, silent streets that are lined with enormous houses. You arrive and he lets you in – and you remember now, as you write this, that your hair was so blonde. He doesn't say much. The halls are lined with those studio photos of families where everyone is grinning and wearing black, with their hands on each other's shoulders.

The impeccable kitchen is huge. He – dark haired, middle aged and soft jawed – leans on the counter drinking coffee, and you stand a little way off, unsure what to do with your bag, so you hold it in front of you. He sips and looks you up and down. His lack of engagement makes you babble. He could smile. He could say something to put you at ease. He could make a joke. Some of them make jokes. This one doesn't give a shit how he is perceived.

He says, 'What do you do?' And you tell him that you're in art college and you want to do sculpture. You waffle on about it and he interrupts you. 'No, what do you *do*?' The air pings and focuses and you stand there with your bag in front of you. You suck it all back in and give him the list of what you do, but it's too late. Your presumption that he was asking you about your life was idiotic, and now you are exposed. You are so naïve, so young and so stupid.

He brings you upstairs into his spare bedroom and doesn't speak on the way. He tells you to take off your clothes, and you do. He sits on the bed and watches. You tell yourself, *It's only an hour, an easy hour for two hundred and fifty quid*. You could leave, but it doesn't enter your mind to do so because you've agreed now, and punters with the personality of a skin disease are just part of the job. So you stay, even though you feel afraid and as if you're see-through. He tells you to get on the bed and turn around. You do what he says. You can't look at him. Objectification is the loss of bodily autonomy, and it can happen in a moment. It can happen with a look, a comment or an order. You are the most objectified you have ever felt.

You let you mind shrink and fold so that it is tiny, tiny, tiny, and you leave your body and think about college, the rest of your day, how you will get home. You're just a character, acting a part. You're not really you right now. It's okay. One of your many personas is not in the room, has not made it up the stairs, but is on her way home. Another has melted out of its body-shell and sits on the windowsill, looking on and laughing at the stupidity of a twenty-one-year-old girl thinking she possesses any power at all, in any part of her life.

I think the men with the studio portraits of their families all wearing one colour would be more appalled than other punters at the prospect of their daughters entering the sex trade. The men with the least respect for escorts are the ones you would least expect to pay for sex, the ones with pictures of their wives and small children in their wallets. Many say that punters are deluded, imagining that the women they are paying want them inside them moments after meeting. I don't think punters are deluded. I think they know exactly what they're doing, and they don't care.

You don't want to have sex with him.

He hits you hard as he has sex with you and you knew this was going to happen because he said he wanted rough sex in his text, so you can't really complain.

It's over, and he doesn't say thank you or goodbye. He grimaces an attempt at a smile as you go out the door.

You get the bus home. It didn't seem as if you made him that happy. You didn't do a good job. You are responsible for the client's enjoyment of the time he spends with you. If a man isn't happy, it's your fault. You have to make him happy. They pay for the type of sex they want, not what you are comfortable with. It isn't about you. Even in a relationship, it can be hard to name your needs and assert your boundaries. But here you are getting paid to please, to endure, to put up with, not to enjoy. As one punter said on one of the online chat forums, 'It doesn't matter if they [escorts] enjoy it or not. All that matters is that they consent to it.'

You feel the stark reality of having had sex with a man you didn't want to have sex with. You have betrayed yourself. You need the punters to make you feel valued, and you hate them when you end up feeling used, discarded and violated. Then you need them more.

This middle-aged man was supposed to treat you like a human being. He was supposed to recognise that you were twenty-one years old, and what that means. If only he had, maybe you wouldn't still recall him in your mid-thirties.

On the bus home, you hold your money, and you feel a little better.

Sometimes you get a sense of imminent violence that doesn't manifest. It is an undercurrent – a sharp tug on your ponytail or a hand placed around your jaw. Not violent enough to put a stop to. There is no way of knowing the man's intentions, so it's easiest and safest to go along with it and prevent things escalating. Just like women do with sexual predators outside the sex trade. You think, *This is going to be a hard one*, and you accept and acquiesce to the hardship. You do this with all men, all the time.

During sex, you are at the mercy of the punter who has paid

to have sex the way he wants. If he says, 'Turn around', you turn around. If he pushes you down for a blowjob, you give him a blowjob. They squeeze your throat. They pull your hair. All of it happens so fast, there is no room for consideration of how you feel. How can you negotiate consent for something that is already happening, has already happened? How can you negotiate consent when you have been paid to do the exact thing you would like to negotiate your way out of?

When it comes to penetration, there is little you can do to physically maintain control. How deep, how fast, it's all up to the man. But why would these men consider what is okay for you? It's like caring that the waitress in the café is really enjoying serving your coffee.

One man leans hard on your chest and you can't breathe. He says things into your ear while crushing you. In the calmest voice you can summon, you ask him to move. This is the reality of paid-for sex. It is not having sexual escapades in which both of you joyfully unravel your sexuality. It's about getting fucked for money and pretending that everything's fine.

There were 'nice' punters too. Beyond the violence of penetrating you for money, most weren't violent. Many were a laugh, and you hung around with them afterwards. It doesn't make what they did okay. In hindsight, it actually makes it worse, the betrayal sharper.

It wasn't sex. Sex is voluntary and sexual consent is flexible and reversible. Sex is freely given and freely expressed. It is not something you have to strategise or *get through* or *get over with*. Not something you have to do to get something. Not something that traumatises. Prostitution sex is not sex. Sex is mutual communication between two people. Sex is something that people create together. What men are paying for is not 'sex', but the use of a woman's body. They are paying their way around sexual consent, paying for the concept of consent. The sex trade is compensated sexual violation.

Our sexuality is inextricably connected to our sense of self and how we express ourselves, how we move through the world. We have sex for lots of reasons – to be kind, to express affection – not always because we're feeling an insatiable urge. But mutuality is still present. Having sex outside these parameters can be destructive and leave us feeling used, empty and depressed. Our bodies absorb the trauma of unwanted sex, even if we agree to it, and money doesn't change that or compensate for it.

Agreeing to something does not make that thing any less harmful for our bodies or minds. It is psychologically exhausting, damaging and toxic to fake a connection to someone, especially a sexual connection. Not being free to be yourself in such a vulnerable and intimate situation is physically and psychologically exhausting. Being paid to have sex on someone else's terms is the farthest thing from sexual autonomy that exists.

Why did I think it was a good idea for me to sell sex? I look back on many relationships and sexual encounters in the same way. How did I think *he* was a good person for me to share my heart with? Why did I put up with sex with that man? This is how we grow, I suppose. We develop new awareness as we age and grow in our self-worth.

I don't know why it confuses me so much; it is all very obvious. I didn't know then what I know now. Our narratives unfold as life goes on, and we experience more, learn new things, and patch up the missing parts of our prior selves. I can see in a new light my consent to what happened to me, with me and by me. I wonder at the meaninglessness of the term 'consent' in sexual experience if we don't ascertain what it means, if we understand it only to mean 'okay'.

It is really hard to articulate the atmosphere that is inherent in a much older, strange man handing you money, taking off his clothes and telling you what sex acts he wants performed on him. It's really hard to articulate the precise and specific pressure, the sense of powerlessness. In prostitution, the woman has no physical or emotional space. The 'client' fills all the space with himself. He can swan about in this space. It is his; he has paid for it. He sits on the bed with his dick in his hand and looks the woman over. He is paying for her to retreat into herself, to be less of herself, to erase herself, to make herself smaller, to submit to his wants. The woman is not authentically there with him. A version of her is undressing in front of him. What he sees is her survival mask. But he doesn't want more. Paying for a body is enough to assure him that what he's doing is okay.

I asked two of the men if they were married. We were chatting while I was getting my things together to leave. They said yes. Between them, they had spent five hundred euro on me. I asked them why they rented escorts. They said it was a fun thing to do. They said their wives wouldn't do what they wanted sexually. I asked them why they didn't talk to their wives about what they wanted. Their eyebrows shot up in bemused surprise at the question – one of them still sitting there naked – and they laughed at me. The idea of what they did in this world being a part of that world was laughable. The idea of being honest was laughable. I was laughing too: the situation was ridiculous. Those men will never be honest with their wives. It's more important for them to feed their sense of sexual entitlement and the power that comes from paying for easy and emotionally void sex.

In the media, the men who pay their way inside women are described by many sex-trade advocates as lonely, elderly, disabled or socially isolated. They are described as men wanting to 'connect', in need of touching a woman's body, wanting a hug, a chat. In the four years I spent 'servicing' random men, I never met any man who just wanted to talk, or needed a hug. Not once. The vast majority were in their forties and fifties, middle class, self assured and heaving with a sense of entitlement. There was no 'crippling shyness' or social anxiety. But even if 100 per cent of punters were wheelchair-ridden, chronically lonely, altruistic philanthropists, they have no right to use a woman's body to have an orgasm. Nothing gives anyone that right. To achieve orgasm is not a right. Sex is neither a bodily need nor a right. Punters can be funny, likeable, generous men. They are also lazy, emotionally immature, co-dependent, selfish and misogynistic. I know this because they pay for sex. No other evidence is needed.

One man comes into the bedroom in his black work suit, says, 'Hi,' and immediately starts taking off his clothes. You smile at him and sit there on the bed in your underwear, waiting. He pushes you back and takes off your knickers. He moves between your legs, and you gesture at the condom waiting on the bedside table, next to the hundred and fifty euro he has given you. 'There's a condom there,' you say, but he ignores you. He pushes your legs apart and shoves his fingers inside you. You are about twenty-three years old; he is in his mid-forties. He behaves as though he is a pushy, horny teenager. He is not someone you want to please, to make happy. He is an entitled jock, your most hated type of man. He sticks his penis inside you, and you shoot backwards up the bed. 'Hey, why don't you put on a condom? You could actually fuck me then.' You keep your tone breezy. You can't let him know you're afraid because then he will have more power over you.

'Sorry,' he says. 'Sorry.'

He sticks himself inside you again and you twist away. 'Just put a condom on. It's right there.' He ignores the invitation and says, 'Sorry.' It seems it is the only word he is capable of saying. Despite understanding that sticking an uncovered penis into a woman is wrong, he keeps doing it. You are worn out with struggling and trying to maintain a jokey façade. The jokey façade is necessary: you don't want to irritate him because he might just rape you with no condom on.

Eventually, he has had enough of dipping in and out of you but getting no satisfaction, and he flips you over onto your stomach. You lie still, expecting him to put the condom on and fuck you, but he wanks all over your back. As he wanks he says, 'I'll be back to you. I'll definitely be seeing you again' and so on and on and, oh god, it's so boring hearing men saying these things.

After he comes, he cannot get out of the room fast enough. He pulls on his clothes and doesn't look at you as you clean yourself up and put your knickers on. He looks like a completely different person. His round, open, wide-eyed face has morphed into a small, crinkled one. He glances at you as he picks up his car keys and mutters, 'I'll text you again.' He's embarrassed to look at you. Many men shift like this afterwards, as if they've just woken up. You're used to it: you're that shameful thing in which they indulge.

I do not want to be writing this. My world is getting smaller. The more I dwell inside this trauma, the less relatable I am to those around me, and the more I withdraw. I cannot be normal. To face relentlessly into the hardest parts of the past means I become colder and closed-off with most people in my life, pulling down the shutters in case they see too much. My world is becoming my home, the kitchen table I write on and my dog's gaze from her bed. This isn't good, and I don't know how to change it.

As I write, I experience waves of dense shame washing over me that I did these things, that I offered myself up for abuse. I was a willing participant. I hated myself that much. When I describe an experience, I write a paragraph or two, then look out the window and see the men in front of me instead of the trees, my neighbour's car, my window boxes.

I feel cold inside, and I'm exhausted nearly all the time. I try not to get lost in it. I do it in small chunks. Sometimes I write for only an hour or two a day, sometimes less. I remember how young I was, how I used to do my hair or dress, or I remember something a punter said to me – his age, his face – and I feel empty, like I'm not really here.

I'm reading *The Places that Scare You* by this Buddhist nun called Pema Chödrön. I found it discarded on the beach with some other books about two years ago, left in a pile by the railway-bridge steps. I picked up the books, brought them to the bench nearby and let the dog off the lead to run around while I looked at them.

The title drew me to it. In her book, Pema writes how in moments of experiencing difficult, scary feelings, we could connect with all the other beings around the world who are feeling or have felt similarly. By default of being human, we have all experienced loneliness, isolation, shame, guilt, regret. The events that might have produced them do not matter because the feelings are universal. I breathe in the feelings of shame or self-doubt or loneliness, connecting with the rest of the world's inhabitants who feel like this, who also stare at the sea or hold their dog, and feel shame or self-doubt or loneliness. And I breathe out compassion for me and everyone else. When I do this, the feeling has less weight and I feel more connected, more on the earth.

I don't want to be known purely for this small part of my life that took place more than ten years ago. This is the hardest part. I want to be known for who I really am, not for the things that happened to me, not for the worst mistake I have ever made. I went to vote in a general election this morning with my dog, and everyone was smiling at us. I like people smiling at me and the dog. I don't want to lose the smiles of the people around me.

The Mariana Trench is in the Pacific Ocean, and is the deepest ocean trench in the world. It was formed when two of the earth's plates collided and one was forced beneath the other. It is 11,034 metres deep, enough to fit Mount Everest with two kilometres to spare, and it is more than five times wider than it is deep. The water at the bottom of the trench has a pressure of eight tons per square inch, making it challenging to explore because there is a risk of implosion. The temperature is just above freezing. There is life in the black-as-night Mariana Trench: snail fish, cucumber fish and amoeba-type creatures. So far only three people have made it to the deepest part. More people have walked on the moon than been down there.

The trench was last explored by the film-maker James Cameron in 2012. I watch his descent online and feel nauseous as he lowers himself into the tiny space in the sea vessel. It takes three hours to get down, and then he spends four hours on the bottom of the trench. It hasn't all been explored yet. There is too much of it. I go down a Google rabbit hole all afternoon and, as I scroll and scroll, I feel more and more frightened and out of my body. I click out and look around me, at my desk, my glass of water, my lip balm.

And once the storm is over you won't remember how
you made it through, how you managed to survive.
You won't even be sure, in fact, whether the storm
is really over. But one thing is certain. When you come
out of the storm, you won't be the same person who
walked in. That's what this storm's all about.

Haruki Murakami, *Kafka on the Shore*

PEOPLE-PLEASER

Sometimes I ask teenage girls hanging around my village how old they are, just to give me a gauge for how I might have looked and acted when I was their age. I eavesdrop on their conversations about teachers, friends and siblings. I try to remember what I would have talked about with my friends when I was sixteen, and cannot. I view the girls with a mixture of awe and suspicion. I pretend I'm researching a book, though I'm not really lying when I say that.

When I was small, I was incredibly shy, and people-pleasing gave me a sense of social and emotional safety. At age six, I was caught out telling two girls that each of their drawings was 'the best'. They confronted me, and I looked back at them blankly. I hadn't intended to be dishonest. I thought I was making them happy. Even at six, other people's comfort came above my integrity, my truth that one painting was very definitely 'the best'.

When I was four or five, on holiday with my family, I got lost in Düsseldorf city centre. We had stopped to look at a window display, and they'd moved off, presuming I was with them. When I realised they were gone, I raced to find them. I waited at traffic lights with the other pedestrians, all giants, still following the rules but crying and desperate to keep running. I ran and I cried. Finally, a Turkish woman grabbed my arm to stop me, took me back to her apartment and called the police. While we waited, she offered me an apple and a Kinder chocolate. I took the apple, even though I was dying for the chocolate. The need to be seen as 'good' was so overwhelming, even when I was lost and in deep distress, that I couldn't accept the comfort of a small bar of chocolate. I don't remember the police coming or seeing my family again. But I can still remember the apartment of the woman who found me, how dark and cool it was, and I remember the apple sitting on the glass coffee-table.

2000

There is a man in my phone.

He sends me text messages.

Nobody knows about him except me.

He is a secret.

Sometimes he texts me a lot for a few days.

At other times he doesn't text at all for months.

Mobile phones are a relatively new concept. Text-messaging is new. The internet and email are new. I'm sixteen. In the park we drink vodka and play snake on our flip phones and compare who has the tiniest mobile. Someone has a magazine and is reading out the personal ads. We find them hilarious, clustering around to mock the authors. It is springtime and I'm sitting on the grass, intrigued by and curious about these personal ads. Most of them are explicit, in that the authors only want sex. *No strings attached. Discretion essential.* They are all men. Sarah and Michelle compose a text to send to one of the phone numbers. It takes ages. Everyone is squealing. We wait. No reply. They text another. Nothing. Disappointment. As usual, I'm watching more than being involved. After a little while they move on. They know it's nonsense.

Everyone but me.

For me this seems like a dark and delicious opportunity to destroy myself a little. My sixteen-year-old self is drawn to the side of a precipice, whatever it may be. I can't help myself. I slide the magazine into my school bag and spend the bus journey home texting these numbers of strange men. Over the next few days, I'm excited when they respond, telling me things, asking me things. I pretend to be all sorts of different people. I'm playing and yet I'm serious. I'm giggling at my phone, feeling high on the sexual power I feel I have over these adult men. I am the owner of a brand-new sexuality and a brand-new power. The power of being wanted is inebriating. Most of the men cop on quickly that I'm not an adult woman, get annoyed and stop texting me. It's okay, though: only one needs to latch on.

One does.

It was stupid teenage behaviour.

It should have been harmless.

J was my secret phone man. He was not threatening. He didn't find me or groom me or infiltrate my family or stalk me online. I went to him. He was in my phone, safe.

He texted me a lot and I loved the attention. Having someone's focus entirely on me was exhilarating. I knew it was shady. I knew he wanted me sexually. I *allowed* it. I *welcomed* it. I didn't put up with it: I *embraced* it into my life. It was worth it. When he texted me, I felt the immediacy of mattering to someone with such intensity. It was like a drug or like buying something expensive that you know you can't afford, a rush of risk, recklessness and surrender. My sexuality mattered. I mattered. Nothing felt as if it had any consequence. I'd sit on my bed hunched over, holding my phone, reading his messages again and again.

He knew I was in school and asked me about my uniform. I pandered to him. I didn't mind. It was worth it for this specific sexual attention. It was normal that men got off on the idea of schoolgirls. I don't know where I'd learned that. I had already absorbed so much without knowing.

I was protected in my home with my family, which made everything else seem safer. I had an expansive internal life, and he was just an addition to it, more private experiences, more private expansion. It was entertaining. And something about this was a balm for how I felt about myself. My new female sexuality felt valuable and fun. It was a secret I enjoyed holding. When you don't have anything to ground you, you can latch on to anything.

J was bossy and authoritative. He called me a 'good girl'. He asked if I'd been good that day. I kind of liked being told I was 'good' a hundred times. If I didn't reply, he wanted to know why. I always replied the way he wanted me to. I didn't question it. I didn't know myself, so it felt easy to be given a role to slip into, instead of feeling lost. Late at night, I sent him text messages, knowing he would reply quickly, knowing I would get the attention I needed. There was a feeling of relief when my phone beeped, a security and escapism in this communication, a zip of excitement.

It was sexual immediately, as I knew it was going to be. He wanted to know what my body was like. He told me about his sexual preferences. He told me what he'd like my uniform to look like, that he already had one for me to wear. He became more demanding. He insisted that I refer to him as 'sir' and, if I forgot, he gave out to me, and I had to apologise.

My phone would beep and I would feel a small knot of dread in my stomach. I would respond to him anyway. Each time I heard a beep, I felt a mixture of anticipation, excitement and fear. I was relieved if it was just a boy I had met at a party. But J wanted me, and I wanted to be wanted so badly, it ached. I knew he was an adult, and that I was younger than him. This granted me sexual power, which I understood without words. He was an adult man who wanted me. I was the one with the power of youth, the gift I could bestow upon him.

The texting eased off a little and life progressed. I continued seeing boys and drinking in parks. I babysat the neighbour's children. I learned how to drive. I wrote a short story about a fox and her cubs. My English teacher gave me an A. I brought the dog out for a walk every morning. I turned seventeen. J blended into the background of my existence. He was white noise, a radio playing low in the background, ice melting in a glass of water.

J wanted to own me, and I wanted to be owned. He asked to meet me, and outlined how he'd like me to behave around him, how I was going to help him realise his fantasies, how he wanted me to look, to dress. It continued like this for many months.

He was providing a secret world where I was viciously desired, but desired all the same. I felt like a prize. His desire for me was flattering and overwhelming. His attention was like a drug. I agreed to meet him. I don't remember agreeing to it. I just remember being there.

After I had agreed, I couldn't change my mind. I couldn't disappoint him; it had been going on for too long to turn back. I had to make him happy. I had such a slight sense of personal agency, of free will, that it was barely existent.

He warned me not to *seduce* him with my *sexy body*.

He warned me that he might get *turned on* by me and not to *take advantage* of my *power* over him. There was significant comfort and security in being told who I was and how to behave.

The house was in the middle of a vast suburban estate, the kind you get lost in and feel like you'll never find your way out of. The kind with enormous flat green areas and screaming children, except there were no screaming children.

J was in his early thirties, I think. It's hard to know. He was tall and skinny with thin, ginger hair and shiny shoes. He had a slightly red-tinged face and a sharp, pointy nose. He was not attractive, but not unattractive. He'd blend in on the street and you wouldn't notice him walking past, even if you were looking out for him. He had a middle-class Dublin accent and dressed in a forgettable bland way to match his forgettable bland face.

He opened the sliding door into his house. He had told me to wear a short skirt and I had complied. It was a fluffy yellow thing. He let me in and didn't smile.

He still lived with his mother, or maybe he was just using the house while she was out. I remember the hallway with stairs to the right and a living room straight ahead. The house was musty, dark and dingy. I sensed something heavy and uncomfortable, but couldn't articulate what it was. It had a bad, claustrophobic feeling. There was stuff on every surface – religious icons and crucifixes, collections of staring eyes, animals and figurines regarding me impassively.

The furniture was mismatched. There seemed to be too much of it, as if someone had just lugged it in and dumped it haphazardly. Old newspapers were piled on couches and chairs. The wallpaper was a pale yellow with a floral pattern. J did not have a good energy, and neither did the house.

He sent me up to the bathroom. I don't remember his voice or his words, but I know he told me to plait my hair. I went up the narrow staircase and took a left into the bathroom. It was tiny, and everything felt plastic and cheap. I did my hair. I didn't mind. I knew he wanted the pornified schoolgirl thing. I was up there for a while, torn between wanting to leave the bathroom and wanting to stay in between before and after.

I came back down.

J was at the bottom of the stairs waiting for me.

He grabbed me by the wrist and dragged me across the living room. His attitude and demeanour had changed. He was meaner now, in my patchy memory – no longer polite. I remember images, the sliding door, his fingers gripping my wrist. I think now, *Did that actually happen? Am I just making it all up? Maybe it wasn't so bad. Was it exploitation if I willingly showed up?* I think, *Why are you making such a big deal out of this?*

I think and I think and I think. I decide this isn't worth writing a book about and stop. I try to do other things with my life, anything, but feel empty and purposeless. I am inevitably brought back to this place.

J dragged me across the room. My insides melted, and I tried to pretend I was okay with it. Going along with things made it hurt less than resisting. And I was his now. I no longer had control. I had never had control. It was a naive, teenage perception that I held some sexual power over him. He let me believe I had power, but he knew I had none.

I knew what his plans were. He had sent me lengthy texts, stories and fantasies about what he'd like to do to me. I knew he wanted to hurt me. I was okay with that because I was drawn to self-harm. *Please, don't let the reward for this be sex.* I hadn't said that was okay. But I'd agreed to be there. I'd agreed.

He told me to take off my underwear, so I did, and he squirrelled it away somewhere and I remember thinking, *Hey, that's mine!* but not saying it out loud. He told me to put my arms up and he took off my top and my bra and then put a white T-shirt on me. It was too small and I felt self-conscious.

I didn't like this man.

I had no idea why I was staying there. I could have just left.

But the thought did not manifest. In this dense, tight space, there was no opening for it.

I'd agreed. I'd said okay.

As soon as I saw him through the sliding glass door, I knew I didn't like him. *You hated him before you met him*, I think, during one of my thinking marathons many years later.

He pushed me against a wall facing into the yellow paper, and I could feel his eyes on my body. I could feel the stare. I felt degraded, and nothing had even really happened yet. I wanted to move like a ghost into the sad wallpaper and through the wall and out the other side into a neighbour's house. Part of me was absorbed into the wallpaper, watching him watching me. He asked me an obscure question and yanked on one plait waiting for an answer. I got it wrong. *Don't touch me*. I felt like my insides were being microwaved.

J teased me about how I looked, what I was wearing. He used one of my plaits to pull me about. He ordered me around, got me into various positions in the jammed living room. He hurt me.

He kept telling me how bold and bad I was. The problem is that I wanted to be degraded. I wanted to be treated badly. I deserved this. I deserved it because I was broken anyway. He wanted the power and he wanted control and I wanted someone to restore me to who I was before, and to tell me that I was *good*, that I was a *good girl*, that I was *okay*.

I went upstairs to put my own clothes back on, but I

realised I didn't have my underwear because he'd taken it. I went back down and he was holding it, waiting. He told me to go back to the bathroom and run it under the tap. I did it because he had told me to.

Then he told me to put it on in front of him, so I did.

I swallowed and felt my jaw clench.

I wish I had shown him how upset I was. But I could endure anything and I had this stubborn thing about not wanting him to see me upset. This was the first time I recognised that a line had been crossed, that this was a humiliation too far. But I was good at ignoring crossed lines. I used to make a humming sound in my head that blocked out the feeling. I thought, *He wants to make you feel bad, so don't let him know you feel bad.*

Sometimes I give talks in schools to transition-year students and I observe the sixteen- and seventeen-year-old boys. I go to the local newsagent, and I see the teenage boys from the neighbouring school. I look at them closely and feel something like nausea. I imagine them walking to school, doing their homework, sending memes to their friends. I see the vulnerability they try to disguise with a fragile front. They seem pretty pure to me. I see the vast potential for harm. How easy it is to harm them. How easy it is for them to harm. I used to be a naive, vulnerable, inexperienced, immature teenager, and before that a child, a toddler, a baby. I wonder what happened to him.

When I was finally leaving the house in the frilly yellow skirt, the wet knickers stuck to me beneath it, J pressed a hundred Irish pounds, two fifties, into my hand.

'Here's some pocket money,' he said, standing at the door to let me out.

I didn't know what to say.

'Oh, okay,' I said.

I took the money and I left, tucking the notes into my bag. I was ecstatic.

A hundred pounds! Just for that?

For a hundred pounds, it was worth it.

I had now been bought off and was muted, rendered silent by all the possibilities one hundred pounds could bring. I was complicit, and I was colluding.

My feelings of fear and of being controlled melted, just like that. All was well. I was in charge. He sent me a text message on my way home. *I hope you're still wearing your wet panties?*

I cringed at his terminology and replied that I was, but I wasn't. I had taken them off and had stuffed them into the bottom of my bag. But I was now paid to please him.

Normal life overshadowed the not-so-normal bits. I went to school, worried about my friends, wrote English essays, drank vodka in parks and took care of the guinea pigs.

I saw J every few months in hotel rooms around the city

centre, and he paid me every time. He wasn't adversely affecting my life in any tangible way, not yet anyway. Others left me mostly alone. I found life lonely, my internal world a refuge. I had reached that point of near adulthood, when you start to think you have to deal with things on your own.

All four of my sisters and brothers had moved away from home, and there was a lot of alone time. I withdrew further into my internal world and became split in two – the outer parts behaving normally and protecting my inner experiences.

J and I never talked about what he wanted me to wear, and we never talked about the money, which was always sitting on top of the clothes, folded on the toilet in the hotel bathroom. The unspoken unspeakable has so much more power and weight than what we allow to air.

It was always the same – a school uniform. It was never a real one but a 'sexy' one: a short plaid skirt, a white T-shirt, knee socks, navy knickers. My hair had to be in plaits. He would direct me into the bathroom, and I would put on the uniform, plait my hair. Now that he was paying me, it was all on his terms, and this happened insidiously, through atmosphere, intonation, silent oppressive expectation and the powerlessness of a teenager in a room with an adult man. It didn't bother me to dress like this, at least not then. I cringed, but found it clichéd and harmless. I was so separate from myself, he could have done anything to me or requested anything from me and I would have done it.

I want this to be fiction, a story I've made up.

I remember getting the DART into town and sitting there watching myself not wanting to be on the DART into town.

I put on the uniform and, with it, the submission. Maybe I wouldn't have done some of the things he wanted if I hadn't been wearing the uniform. It helped him to see me in this role, a character. It helped me to see myself in this role.

I feel something like fear or dread or unease writing this down, as if I am there now with him, as if I am made of glass. I feel uprooted, at risk and unsafe, like anything could happen to me. I remember the scratch of the navy knickers he made me wear.

He was right and I was wrong, and he had to correct me all the time and teach me how to be good. That was how he spoke to me, as though he was my teacher, imparting wisdom, giving out to me, sighing, rolling his eyes, exasperated. I was a stupid little slut, and he was the responsible adult trying to teach me where I was going wrong. I didn't reply to his texts fast enough; I was always late; I was not dressed how he liked; my plaits were not done.

He spoke to me as if I was a child, using child language. He gave me instructions. 'Now you're going to be a good girl and get up on the bed for me. Turn around. Open your legs ... That's it, good girl. Open your legs wider for me. What are you? That's right, you're a very bold girl.'

He hurt me in various ways, and I wanted my body to hurt

because it eased the guilt. He hurt me in ways I was not okay with, and I allowed it. I sensed a toxic, putrid dirt. I could taste it, but I could not name it. And I was here now. I'd agreed. Maybe *I* was the dirt.

If I was naked, he wouldn't let me cover myself. He told me to put my arms down. He looked me over with his small eyes and he *drank* me in. He devoured all of me, every part of me. My body was not mine. I shivered out of my skin. My body was his – it was anyone's.

We were in a hotel in Dublin city centre and he told me to go over beside the window, which looked out on the car park. He told me that anyone who glanced up would see me naked. I stood there. He took off my clothes gradually, slowly spreading out his ownership of me. My consent or desire or lack thereof was immaterial. When he had finished, he told me what a good girl I was, and I felt a surge of perverse pride, because I had done something right.

Maya Angelou wrote: 'At fifteen, life had taught me undeniably that surrender, in its place, was as honourable as resistance, especially if one had no choice.' I suppose I learned to surrender because I never felt I had a choice. I surrendered into my body's role as being for men's pleasure.

J liked the ritual and routine of it. Putting me in the uniform. Undressing me in stages. Putting me into different positions. Ordering me about in his fake boss-man voice. It was structured and organised. He liked it so much that he started emailing me exactly what would happen the next time he saw me.

He was in charge, his tiny ego swelling and bursting inside him. He chose increasingly explicit positions for me that became more uncomfortable as time went on. He enjoyed finding new positions to put me in that were difficult to keep. If I moved, he had another excuse to hurt me.

While he did things to me, I focused on the headboard of the bed or the beige carpet of the hotel room or on his shoes or the curtains. I was a stubborn, sullen teenager around him. He poked and prodded at me, trying to annoy me, trying to force his way past this façade. He got too close, slithered up behind me, pulled my head back with my hair and whispered things into my ear. Sometimes he asked a question and yanked on a plait so I'd have to answer him, acknowledge him. 'Hmm?' Yank. 'Hmm?' Yank, yank.

'Such a filthy girl,' he'd say. 'You're a dirty little slut,' he'd say. 'What are you?'

'I'm a dirty slut,' I'd say. 'I'm a bad girl. I'm a whore.'

I said whatever he wanted me to say, all the insults to do with being a woman. He smacked me between my legs and around my thighs with a riding crop. He pretended he was going to hit me really hard, and I winced and braced myself. He chuckled. A second later, he hit me really hard.

'Look at me,' he said.

I looked at him.

It brought all of me to one place. It forced me to acknowledge and experience this pain. Mental and physical pain compounded into one. Forced intimacy that is not intimate. My face froze into numbness. A new skin grew over my eyes, so I could look at him and not really look at him, so I could see without seeing. The damage was not physical pain, but the quieting of my mind to stay still and yield and ignore the smaller part of me that knew this was wrong.

I was so controllable because I needed so much.

I was a wanted thing.

I tasted this knowledge and it was intoxicating.

My memories of this man are few, but they all sit together, like stacked books pressing down on a shelf. Some of the memories are of his voice or my feelings, or are still images or textures.

When I look back at this jumble of situations, chronology can stop making sense. I have to try to pin down events to what year I was in at school, what friends I had at the time, if it was before or after other significant occasions. I get confused. Sometimes I think I know something to be absolutely true, then realise something else again. I don't trust my memory. It's hard to know when things happened, what age I was, where they took place. I remember bits here and bits there.

Trying to pick them apart means trying to pick pain apart. It means reflecting with concentration on each detail. This is impossible. Thinking about it makes me want to shove myself to the farthest part of the room I am currently in. It makes me want to wrench off the parts of me that he touched. I can't be a part of *here* while I am *there*. I tell myself: *This is the last time you have to do this.*

I do not remember the first time he took photos of me, but after that his tripod and big camera and leads were all set up in the hotel room every time. It was never discussed. It was just all set up. If you have ever been in the company of cameras and tripods, you will understand how intimidating it can feel. I have no idea how I felt about the camera on its tripod. I have no idea how I felt about anything. I accepted and relented and allowed and pleased.

He put me into a position he liked and took some photos. Then, he changed my position and took more. He had a lead attached to the camera so that he could take a photo while he was doing something to me.

I hated it. I didn't look at the camera. I tried to hide my face.

It is difficult to explain how it felt when I heard the flash. It was like cold water gushing under translucent skin. It felt more exposing than taking off my clothes ever did. I didn't want any of this to be happening to me, but I couldn't stop it. The words for how I felt were lodged, like mud, in the back of my closing throat. *It'll be over in an hour*, I told myself. *It's only time. Time passing can't hurt you. It'll be over in an hour.* My stomach sank and tightened and I endured. I didn't know how to say no.

Once or twice, I showed him that I was upset. I mumbled, 'I don't want to.' He sat down at the edge of the bed and pulled me onto his lap. He wrapped his arms around my waist. I perched on him, hating him, hating my nakedness, hating how immobile I was and how I was unable to stop anything when it had started, hating how much I wanted to please him. I could feel his bony legs underneath me and I could smell his smell. He held me tight and talked to me in that voice you use when you talk to small children. It was a reassuring voice. I nodded. He talked quickly and didn't ask me any questions or let me say anything, and he encouraged me back onto the bed.

Another time, I came out of the hotel bathroom and found him hiding a video camera underneath a shelf. I managed to get out the word 'No.'

Then, he put pictures of me on the internet. Initially, I did not recognise my own body in them. When I did, I felt sick and, acting on autopilot, I managed to get them deleted. His email to me was furious. He mocked my feelings and dismissed me. *No one is bothered by a couple of pictures of a naked girl on a bed. You can't see your face.*

I got used to the photo-taking because you can get used

to anything. I took the money, bought stuff with it and felt better.

One day, I was waiting outside a hotel J had never taken me to before. It was a big old posh one. I was about eighteen. I remember my reluctance and that I was wearing a white floaty top with big wide sleeves, which I loved. He immediately gave out to me in his boss-man voice that what I was wearing was see-through (it wasn't) and said it was slutty.

He made me carry his briefcase into the hotel, and I followed him. We waited in reception and I wanted to die. I looked up at the receptionist behind the enormous dark wooden desk and felt like I was in a film. I had to look away from her. I wanted her to ask me if I was okay, if I needed anything, if I knew what I was doing. In my memory, the reception counter was huge – I could barely see over the top. I kept looking down, like a child waiting for her father to be finished checking in. The receptionist carried on, unalarmed. She and he chatted to each other casually while I stood next to them, between worlds. Years and years later on my way home from work, I went into the hotel and checked: it was just a normal-sized desk.

I couldn't endure my heart pounding any longer. I slid off to the ladies' room, locked myself into a cubicle and examined my chipped nail polish. I thought about my then boyfriend. I wanted him to come and take me home on the train. I sat down and contemplated calling him. *No, I couldn't. What would I say? I couldn't bring this into his life. He wouldn't understand, and then he'd break up with me, and I'd have no one.*

J was out there in reception, probably annoyed at the delay. I wouldn't be able to get past him. He knew where I was. I knew instinctively that telling him I wanted to leave wouldn't work. There was no way I could have said, 'Actually, I'm going home.' It was unthinkable. There was nothing to do but hide in the cubicle, adrenalin rushing in waves through my body, urging me to do something, move in some direction, but I couldn't. I was trapped.

Eventually, I sent J a text message, telling him I didn't want to go up to a room, and that I would do anything else he wanted. Not an outright no. I couldn't say *no*. He rang me many times and I didn't answer. I don't remember what happened after that.

I might not have said no.

I didn't say *I don't want to* or *Please stop*, but I showed him 'No.' I showed him *I don't want to*. I showed him discomfort, reluctance and unwillingness. I showed him 'No' so many times.

I was about nineteen when J asked me to meet a 'friend' of his. I don't remember him saying it, but I knew I would get paid. It was an easy way to make a hundred pounds. It was only an hour of my time. It was just time passing. Time passing could not hurt me. And then I'd be outside again with money to hold in my hands.

I arrived at the hotel and hovered outside, looking up at the windows. I was nervous. I didn't want to go up the little path to the entrance. I could feel my heart banging inside me, but I'd agreed to go and it was organised now, so I couldn't turn back. If I left now, I wouldn't get the money that made me feel better, which was now the whole point of it.

This felt like a real job, not like meeting J. This was different. This was an agreement in which the payment was explicit. I had a name, a place and a time to be there. The man who opened the hotel-room door was old, with white hair and a wrinkled face. My stomach churned. I felt a hint of something. I swallowed it. *This was happening.*

The old man was excited and talkative and ushered me in, acting as if everything was fine. We had all consented.

He had lingerie on the table and gestured for me to put it on. When I came out of the bathroom wearing the garish pink knickers with tie-up sides and an equally garish pink camisole top, he was sitting in a chair, beaming.

'Walk around the room,' he said, and I did.

'Walk slower!' he bellowed.

I walked slower.

'Sexier!'

I walked more slowly and awkwardly around the small room, back and forth in front of him. I didn't know what he meant by 'sexier'.

He sat in his chair and watched.

'I'll buy you something different to wear for the next time,' he said. 'Or I can give you money to buy something yourself.' He was chirpy.

He told me to get on the bed and then he sat right down beside my face. I felt the lightness I was so familiar with, as if my body weighed nothing, like I wasn't really there.

He turned me over and rubbed my entire body very gently. For some reason gentle touches were so much more difficult to experience than hard ones. I closed my eyes and shoved my face into the bedclothes. I could hear something, the whoosh of a belt coming off, and a wall of anxiety hit my chest. *It's going to happen now*, I told myself. *He's going to have sex with you. This old man is going to have sex with you.* But he didn't. He hit me all over my body with his belt. He opened my legs and hit me there. The pain took my breath away. He took off the top and knickers and continued to hit me. I made a small noise on an exhalation, and I remember that he let out a soft chuckle.

He threw down the belt and pushed my legs further apart, and again I thought, *Okay, it's happening now. He's going to have sex with you.* But he didn't. Instead, he shoved his fingers inside me so hard that I held my breath and clutched the bedclothes. This pain was so much worse than the earlier pain. I squeezed my legs together, but he pulled them apart again. It felt like he was digging my insides out. I had no words, no sounds and no power. I had nothing. I was nothing.

'You're not very wet,' he said. 'But you're very tight.'

He pulled out his fingers, and I felt ragged. He told me not to move and he left me on the bed. I heard him sitting down in the chair. I heard him rustling about, and realised that he was masturbating.

I waited, tense and miserable. With his orgasm would come freedom, money, and the tiny kick that I'd done my job and was valued for it. All I needed was that tiny kick to feel okay. I just had to keep thinking of him as a sad old man for another few minutes. I could feel his eyes on me.

This was not the same as J. This was different. I had a sort of relationship with J. I saw him regularly. I knew him in a context where, although he objectified me, I was a person and he was a person. This was a stranger. We had no relationship. A stranger was touching me and doing what he wanted to me. A stranger had had his hand inside me and didn't ask me if I wanted that. He felt entitled to do what he wanted with my body.

That moment, on the bed staying still because I was told to, with that old man wanking behind me, was how I became an 'escort', even though I didn't know it. That was the exact moment it happened.

And now I was a prostitute, a 'sex worker'.

Without knowing it.

Without agreeing to it.

It happened just like that.

When it was over, I put my clothes back on, he gave me the money and I left.

I told J that I didn't like the meeting, but I downplayed it. I was still colluding with him, and therefore with his friend. If an abuser is any good at abusing, he will make you feel like you're part of it, like you're in on it. I guess I *was* in on it. I told him that the old man was too rough.

'I'll talk to him,' he said.

His mild surprise at the old man's behaviour made me believe that in some tiny way he valued me. The problem was that our interpretation of the word 'value' was very different.

The thing that stuns me when I think back on it, on multiple levels, is the ages of those two men. I catch myself in disbelief and breathe deeply. Mid-thirties and maybe mid-sixties. I was a teenager, barely an adult. They had the life experiences of sorrows, joy, fury, hurts, devastation, loss, insight and wisdom which come with age. I try to re-form it in my mind so that they were unaware of the harm they were causing, unaware of the vulnerability of my youth. But the hard, difficult truth is that they wanted me because I was so young, because I lacked life experience, because I was so vulnerable.

When I ask the teenagers who gather at the newsagent's in my village how old they are, I think I'm trying to make my youth more real to myself, to reassure myself, to forgive myself.

The object of writing is to write to yourself, to let yourself know what you have been trying to avoid.

Bessel A. van der Kolk, *The Body Keeps the Score*

LOVE AND DEATH

Falling in love, especially when you have no idea what falling in love feels like, is exhilarating. I was seventeen when I met my first boyfriend, D. It was spring or summer, and I was in a friend's back garden drinking and smoking, and he was there too. I'd already heard about him, and maybe seen him around, but I'd never spoken to him. I saw him sitting at the garden table, and I knew he was for me, in the way you know things. We talked that night a lot, sitting close together. We had our first kiss in my car after a party a few weeks later.

Then nothing happened for ages. I heard that he'd kissed someone else, and I was devastated. But then, finally, on the bus back from a trip to Donegal, he gave me his bright red hoodie to wear, and I knew that meant something. He kissed me, and I said, 'Are you mine?' And he said he was. We spent two years together until I broke his heart.

He'd been in a relationship already. He knew what he was doing, and I'm sure it was obvious that I didn't. I had no idea what a sexual relationship entailed. He didn't try anything – he was patient and safe. We had sex for the first time in his bedroom and I remember thinking, *So this is what it's supposed to be like.* But also, *Is this it? Is this all it is?* It was so normal and undramatic that it was nearly boring. I remember his bed, the shafts of light coming in under the curtains onto the sheets, the daylight we were keeping at bay.

We fell in love. He adored me. We rode our bicycles and went on picnics. We collected shells and stones at the beach. We drove to Mayo, and I smoked weed for the first time and got sick, and he had to look after me all night. He always had small gifts he'd found or made for me. He'd make drawings of my name and give them to me on my birthday or on Christmas or Valentine's Day. I still have some things he gave me, hidden in a box full of old feelings I can't bear connecting with. He loved me just as I was.

I reflect on that experience sometimes and know: *This happened. You were loved by a kind and gentle man. This can happen again. Gentleness is a thing you are capable of receiving.* I close my eyes and say thank you to D, wherever he is in the world now.

You might imagine that this boy would have put an end to the J situation but he didn't. J was in my life sporadically throughout that relationship. When I look back on this time, although the two lives ran simultaneously, I can see D on one path and J on the other, two separate strands. There is a disconnection; the memories don't mix. I think secret things have to close themselves off in compartments in your mind to remain secret. I didn't let J into that part of my life. I protected it from him.

I have a memory of where my two lives slid past each other. I was in the city centre with my boyfriend. I said goodbye to him on the street. I watched that sensitive eighteen-year-old boy disappearing, and I went around the corner to the hotel where J was waiting for me, like the earth's plates shifting past each other at a hair's-breadth distance. I could disconnect each thing so that they belonged in different worlds, made of different feelings, different realities, unidentical versions of myself.

If I was looking to feel wanted, why didn't my boyfriend fulfil that? What was going on with me that I needed such an unhealthy situation? Why was I drawn to the dark parts of myself that wanted to harm me? Was it a search for something within myself? Was I self-sabotaging?

I don't have the answers.

During my relationship with D, I was torn between feeling that I was not good enough and feeling that my boyfriend was not good enough because if he was, he wouldn't love me. How could he love me? There had to be a trick in there somewhere. There had to be a reason why someone was being loving, and it couldn't just be because I was worth being loved.

I felt I had to trade something for acts of love. I would

regularly try to catch out my boyfriend in a created transgression. I could make a fight or pick at him until he became angry with me and then, the pure relief of it. *Aha! You don't really love me after all! I was right!* What a triumph to 'confirm' that what I suspected was actually true. I was hard work. I couldn't accept real love. It was too unfamiliar and unpredictable and I was highly strung, waiting to be criticised or told where I was going wrong.

I tried to take my life when I was eighteen years old. I had just finished school. I don't remember much about the weeks beforehand except that I had been planning to kill myself for a long time. When I was trying to remember what to live for, I wrote my boyfriend's name down on my list in my diary, in big capital letters and surrounded it with hearts.

I didn't actually want to die, but I was in crisis – and I was lacking enough connection in my life to survive the crisis. That is all it takes. You don't have to be mentally ill to be suicidal. You don't have to be depressed. You just have to be under-resourced in a crisis.

I wanted to stop. I wanted the feelings of being trapped under the weight of so much pain to stop. I wanted to hold the world still, pause my whole being. I didn't consider asking for help because I didn't feel connected to a life. I experienced it with some curiosity from behind a glass wall, an outsider, a spectator. I was so curious about existence, and regarded my own as something I could hold lightly, decide on a whim to continue or not.

Going to school every day had given me an anchor to a life, an attachment to a structure where I could go and be distracted and focus for long periods. Now I was unattached, floating in space, and there wasn't enough to keep me connected to the earth. I felt the excruciating loneliness of a disconnected life. I didn't know who I was, and I didn't know why I was.

I felt guilty for wanting to die, because a person looking in would see a privileged middle-class good life in a happy family. They would see a kind boyfriend. I was so good at keeping my internal life private and faking being fine that nobody suspected there was anything wrong with me. Besides my boyfriend, I didn't have close relationships, no one I could trust. I didn't want to create problems for my parents, who had given me so much. I was the peace-maker, the one who pre-empted problems. I could not be the source of the problem. I lived inside my own mind, high-walled, sweeping and expansive, which I could inhabit for ever. The exterior – my body, my face, my voice – didn't give much away.

I am still challenged by my internal world. I find it next to impossible to put some things into words. I get a sense of something, a vague taste of its quality, and no words to communicate it. It's a bit like when you have a confrontation with someone and, after it has passed, you come up with the devastating riposte that wasn't available to you minutes earlier – except that this is about everything. I have to sit with these tastes and sensations for some time, until they reveal themselves in words to me, and then the chance to express myself is over.

I find it so hard to take part in panel discussions because I go blank when I'm asked a question. I have to think deeply on everything. I always thought I was a bit thick, especially when I was a teenager, but now I know that I am a sensitive, intuitive person, and that everyday experiences can be more loaded and complex. There is more to process in every encounter, and it takes time for things to land in a way that is accessible. I am both grateful for my rich internal life and dismayed by it. It feels nourishing but it also feels isolating.

My boyfriend spent all his free time with me during these darkest weeks. When he went to Northern Ireland to visit his family, I was waiting at Connolly station when he got back. We went to the beach, we went to the pier, we drove around aimlessly. We walked to the top of Bray Head. He popped up with picnics and presents. He hugged me and asked me not to kill myself. I told him I would try not to. Every night, he called me just before I went to sleep. He stayed on the phone until I was fading with exhaustion. The memories of him make me feel warm.

Wanting to kill yourself, really wanting not to exist any longer, is a greyness that filters into every aspect of your life. I felt as if I was grey and the world was grey and that both of us would be grey for ever. And I felt erased, as if I was hollow, made of my skeleton and skin and nothing else – a walking void. I went through the motions of everyday life, speaking, smiling and laughing when it was expected of me.

The night I attempted suicide, I rang my boyfriend. I don't remember what we talked about. He heard that I was upset and asked me if I had done something, and I told him, yes, I had, and I started to panic, becoming hysterical, telling him I loved him.

He woke his mother and she called an ambulance. It came quietly with blue lights flashing on the driveway. My parents woke up. I know they were there, but I don't remember them being with me. I think I've blocked it out. It hurts too much to think of them waking up, their dawning realisation of what I had done and the pain it inflicted on them.

I remember the feeling of surrendering control to all the adults around me, and it felt like relief. In the hallway,

I held a bag the paramedics gave me to vomit into. I can remember the crisp paper in my hands, the plastic ring on the top of it.

I don't remember the journey to the hospital. I woke up in different places, including the emergency room where a doctor and his team of student doctors came around and pulled the sheets off me and prodded my legs and didn't tell me what was happening. None of them looked me in the eyes. The team asked the doctor questions. I wanted to tell them I was there, but I was unable to speak. Then I was in a storage room full of machinery. I opened my eyes and saw a tiny vase of yellow flowers on a shelf beside me and knew my mother had been there. I remember my limp body. My breath was the only thing I could focus on and I clung to it, breathing in and breathing out, slow and rasping on every exhalation. I have never been so much at the mercy of others.

Then I was in a ward and feeling a little better. In moments of profound pain, my internal world became much more comfortable. There was no need to speak: words had stopped mattering. There were no words for what was happening to me anyway. Words always seemed inadequate as a vehicle for the feelings I had. I enjoyed being looked after in the very basic ways you are looked after in hospital, your physical needs attended to by smiling nurses. A blonde female psychologist came around, but I have no memory of our conversation.

D flouted the rules for visiting hours and came every morning at seven thirty because he knew that was when they woke me up. He brought me lollipops from the hospital shop and sat on my bed and gave me big smiles. The love he had for me poured out of his eyes, and I couldn't say anything. I couldn't match his love with mine.

People are scared even to say the word 'suicide', scared to talk about it, scared to ask questions. Adults are awkward and don't know what to say. More than anything else, I think we're afraid of realising our own inadequacy in these situations, our own unfamiliarity with it, the fear of this unknown dark thing, fear of getting an answer we don't want to hear, fear of saying the wrong thing.

But this boy knew me and he loved me and he wasn't scared of me. D lay down beside me in the dark and stayed with me, so I wouldn't be on my own. This was the greatest gift he could have brought me in those three days I was in hospital, sitting in fearless silence, allowing empty space to fold around me as I reoriented to my life.

To recover from a suicide attempt is complicated. You don't survive an attempt and then immediately want to live again. You don't wake up and feel grateful for your life. You have to recover from the profound act of violence you have enacted upon yourself. The part of you that wants to live has to forgive and integrate the part that wants to die. The part that wants to die has to forgive the part that wants to live. You have to find a way to bring them back together. You have to find a way to hold in one place the disappointment that you are still alive with the relief that you are still alive. You have to find a way to relate to the people who love you and who are afraid of you and who don't know what to say or do, who say the wrong thing or try to control you. You have to forgive them. You have to forgive yourself. You have to find a way to live. You have to start seeing the future as a real thing. It is not easy. Only one thing is clear: from that moment on, things are never going to be like they were, and there is some comfort in that.

I came home from hospital and life went on as normal. I did a course of group therapy, during which the psychiatrist told me I was attention-seeking because I didn't speak. I was so eager to 'heal', so eager to do 'recovery' properly, so naive to think that everything would now change. I would recover, I would be fixed, people would listen to me. But the break-times and lunch-times with the group were more healing than any actual group work.

The silence around my suicide attempt got more comfortable over time until it was a soft, oversized dressing-gown I slipped into for comfort, rather than the claustrophobic, too hot, too scratchy thing it was to begin with. Everything fell back into place.

One night, I was on the phone to D in the kitchen, and he started to cry. We weren't even talking about me nearly dying. He almost choked on his tears. For the first time, I realised that I had profoundly hurt him. I had really hurt someone who loved me. I had maybe even damaged him. The girl he loved had tried to kill herself, come close to dying, and I hadn't yet acknowledged this pain that was separate and different from my own.

Depression and suicide are so inadvertently, unintentionally and unconsciously self-absorbed. I sat there and listened to him sobbing. I allowed myself to witness his feelings. After that phone call, I no longer wanted to die.

Trauma is hell on earth. Trauma resolved is a gift from the gods – a heroic journey that belongs to each of us.

Peter A. Levine, *Waking the Tiger*

STUPID GIRL

After leaving school, I went to University College Dublin to study English but dropped out before the year was through. The college was too big, too populated and too anonymous for a hyper-sensitive person like me. I was accepted to the National College of Art and Design in Dublin, and moved into the city centre.

The relationship with my boyfriend ended, slowly and without any specific turbulence. I had outgrown it. He never knew about J, and I never felt any guilt about not telling him. I wasn't being unfaithful to him: it was something that was occasionally done to me and something that I had normalised. I had created a layer in my life that was completely separate from everything else. The difficulty was being unable to see that it was a problem.

Cycling over the cobblestones in NCAD to get to the Fine Art building felt like a daily home-coming. It was a community, and I belonged to it. It was safe there. Being surrounded by other artists was special, people who were open to the weird conversations, who could sit with the insecure unease that the first stages of creating something bring up, people who accepted you as an artist. I was able to express parts of myself safely, and allow others to experience those parts. I had found a home inside myself.

It is difficult to write about this time of my life because, even though my two worlds coexisted, I do not want to associate that part with J. I want to keep them shut away from each other.

When I think of my time in NCAD, I think of my gentle and funny tutor, the late James O'Nolan – showing him my notebooks, desperate for his encouragement. I think of Pat the caretaker with his smiling eyes and white hair. I think of my art – enormous installations that I wouldn't have the courage to create now. I remember the wood and metal workshops, the technicians John and Brendan and their easy banter, the smell of welding, the feeling of sawdust on my skin. I think about my thesis, which was about the work of Bruce Nauman and his terrifying clowns. I think of the friendships I had, how inclusive and considerate we were of one another. I do not want to infect it with J, but he was in my life then too, so I have to integrate them.

He wasn't around for months and months, maybe even a year went by, and then he seemed to slip back in. I have very little memory of him not being there or being there. He was not integrated with the rest of my life. The memories of my first boyfriend trigger vague memories of other places, people and situations. Those times have a context that is wider than the individual memory. A layered and textured picture is created. But when I remember incidents with J, all I remember is that image. It is so separate in my mind. This is what trauma does. Trauma memories stay detailed and clear. I can guess my age if I remember what hair colour I had, or something like that. But mostly I remember those encounters as isolated incidents that float in this parallel universe and cannot be pinned down to any timeline. I know that J was in the background of my life from when I was aged sixteen to twenty. I remember him being in my life, then not being in my life, then being in my life again, and finally being out of it properly. I don't remember how he seeped back in.

I saw him sporadically – sometimes not for months, sometimes weeks – it depended on his mood, how horny he was. If I didn't hear from him for a few months, I felt a sense of rejection and craved feeling valued and important again. My quickest fix was J's attention. He liked it when I texted him, wanting to see him. Sometimes I sent him a text just to get a reply, and then wouldn't bother meeting him, which infuriated him.

Life had a different kind of energy to it. By the time I was twenty, he was becoming a chore. It had been three years of this. I was no longer afraid of him or intimidated by him. His emails and texts were merely annoying. In college, I could have as much random sex with men as I liked, getting the attention I felt I needed in a much easier and mostly less harmful way.

I started to cancel meeting J. I still met him every now

and then, because it had become a job, a handy way to get a hundred quid. But the money was starting to feel not worth it. I still went along to get it, to pick it up off the school uniform and stuff it into my bag.

When I cancelled J and saw him afterwards, anger poured from his entire lanky body. He invested a lot in meeting me: he had to pay for hotel rooms, he had often taken an unpaid day off work (this was how much he valued me). I used to cancel at the very last minute, sometimes when he was already in a hotel room waiting for me. All day, I'd try not to think about going there. As the time to leave crept closer, the ball of anxiety I was so accustomed to would become tighter and harder inside me. And when I could take it no longer, I would text him some lame excuse or just not show up. The fact that I didn't see him so often meant that it never became overwhelming for me. I became inured to it, and because he never penetrated me, I could believe it was okay. It wasn't *rape*. If he had been nicer to me, the later impact would have been worse, the confusion more difficult to untangle. I was being exploited and valued at the same time. The two merged. Like when I got cat-called in my school uniform by passing vans. It felt good and it felt bad.

J was still in control when I was in his immediate presence. I left college early one day and he picked me up in his car. (I pressed my entire self against the inside of the car door, the air between us tense. I stared hard out of the window.

I stared at the wing mirror.) He took me to his house and forced me into uncomfortable positions so he could get the photo he wanted.

From the moment of taking the money and putting on the school uniform, I was tethered to the feeling of submission to him, the feeling of *I have to* and a sense of loyalty. I felt free when I was not around him physically, and unfathomably trapped when I was in his presence, my self erased.

Once, I tried to get out of doing stuff by offering him oral sex instead. It would be over faster, and maybe it wouldn't involve humiliating me. Most importantly, it was my idea, my terms. It was something I could do, an action I could take. I would have control. I wrote to him that maybe I could do *that* instead of meeting him for the usual two hours. He didn't reply. I met him soon after and he didn't look at me. He mumbled, 'What's all this now about a blowjob?' Some vulnerable thing slipped out in his voice, a shyness, his shame lying underneath. He wanted it. He was awkward. Maybe it was embarrassing for him. Maybe he felt awkward because he liked to dictate what was going to happen to my naked body, while his was always kept private and concealed beneath clothes, and I'd turned things around by taking charge. I'd never experienced him like that before. This was a weird, painful, unspoken moment of exposure for him, and it was also that for me. The irony is that if he had demanded oral sex from me at any point, I probably would have done it.

One morning, I woke up and remembered I had to meet him. I felt the familiar dread and said to myself, *Fuck it.* I was hungover, and I wasn't even going into college. I sent him a text saying I wouldn't make it. I felt some anxiety and swallowed it. I told myself, *He can only affect you when he's with you. It's okay. You are not obliged to do anything.*

Later that morning I was in my bedroom when the doorbell rang. I ignored it. I could already hear one of my housemates going to answer it. Then I heard animated talking. J was barking at her – at least in my memory he was – and then she was in my doorway looking at me carefully and saying that some really angry guy was looking for me. My insides contracted. I didn't know how to cover this up and I was scared.

At the door, he started giving out to me straightaway. He grabbed my wrist hard. 'What's this?' he hissed, pointing to a new tattoo. He didn't like tattoos. He told me I was a stupid girl. He told me it was disgusting. I wondered if he was going to drag me into his car. He was furious with me. In a low, intense voice, he began a litany of complaints about all the times I had cancelled. I was disrespecting him. He had made arrangements. I couldn't keep treating him like this.

I was stuck at the door but I was also not there. I watched him. I watched the lines on his small face and how they moved around his mouth and his eyes. I watched his receding hairline move with his forehead. I watched his mouth open and close and his teeth behind his lips and his small eyes and his red skin.

I looked down and I looked away. I was frozen on the small step of the house. He left in a huff. I closed the door and breathed again.

My housemate came back, wanting to know what was up. I made up something. A mix-up. An acquaintance. She had that face on her when you know someone doesn't believe you. This was different. She was used to me messing around the house, sitting on the couch, making my budget meals, giving out about college, tutors and essays, making her laugh. This was a new experience of me, a revealing of something. I needed to hold it all down.

J emailed, saying he would have sex with me at our next meeting. I read and re-read the email and my insides twisted. I only had sex with those whom I wanted to, not him, with his receding ginger hair, skinny frame and pale freckles on his arms. Not him, with his shrivelled personality, not if he paid me a thousand pounds. I was sure about it. There was no way that was going to happen. Somewhere along the way, I realised I no longer had to do what he wanted.

He probably thought he had gained a little leverage with his latest ploy because I was afraid of him turning up on my doorstep. He probably thought I would be compliant again, but he was wrong. He never should have invaded my normal life, my separate life. He never should have done something that would mean someone in my life would look at me in the careful way my housemate did. I don't think he had any awareness of how terrifying he was to me now and that terror, that near-merging of my secret world and my normal one, had made me see the light. I didn't see him again.

I struggle with the choices I made. I blame myself. I blame him. I blame us both. I write a list in a notebook, which I hide in a drawer to help me remember that it wasn't an equal relationship between two consenting adults.

'He knew exactly what he was doing,' I say to my therapist, C, one day.

A few weeks later, C says it back to me, but I no longer believe it.

'I showed up every time.'

'I was giving him very confusing messages.'

'I could have just stopped.'

I have done courses and workshops and read countless books on sexual trauma and its impact. I work with people every day who hold the same self-defeating trauma beliefs that I have and I do not accept them as valid. Even with all this knowledge and insight, fifteen years later, I look at my therapist, thinking he's just saying these things to make me feel better and I was an idiot teenager who was led on an older man.

In some ways suffering ceases to be suffering at the moment it finds a meaning, such as the meaning of a sacrifice.

Viktor E. Frankl, *Man's Search for Meaning*

POSSUM

I avoid the Temple Bar area of Dublin city at night because I have to fight my way through Brazilian men wearing sandwich boards covered with dated images of almost naked women advertising nearby strip clubs. Sometimes I speak with them, and their humour and ease are jarringly at odds with the images they are draped with. They say they don't like it, but they need to earn money.

The renting of women's bodies is so normalised that tourists and locals alike fail to register the images as they pass. Nobody sees a problem. Nobody cares.

When I get the rare chance, I cover one or two of the naked bodies with anti-porn stickers and vanish before the guy catches me. It gives me great joy to see the sandwich boards again, still bearing the white patches from failed attempts to peel away the stickers.

2004

In the living room, watching television, my housemate Brian comments on an actress: 'She looks like she'd cry during sex.'

'Ha!' I say. 'Yeah.'

I feel a small glow of pride that I'd never succumb to that kind of weak emotional state.

In college, there was a lot of drinking, drugs and sex. Being offered an ecstasy tablet was as normal as someone giving you a cigarette. MDMA offered me the chance to let go of the control I held tightly around me, and experience letting go in a contained, time-limited way. It was a carefully controlled freedom, where I could lose myself in the varying techno beats and dark rooms and allow myself to be swallowed, the edges of myself blurring into others, safely contained in those impermanent chaotic confines. The drugs didn't help my weakness to feel that men wanted me sexually. Ecstasy made me feel as if I was in love with everyone. Apart from outright creeps, I had sex with almost anyone who wanted to have sex with me. I never felt shame about it. Here was a chance to connect with another human being in the most private and vulnerable way, a chance to see them and for them to see me. A chance to know someone in this brief, temporary, fragile way. I valued the honesty of it. Most of those encounters were friendly; some were not. The meaner the sex, the better I felt it suited me, the more I felt I deserved it.

Sometimes there was sadness or loneliness emanating from either of us, and I worked harder to be whatever I sensed the man wanted me to be. *Love me*, I invited them, *or at least love this*, offering my body to them. Sometimes I used sex as a form of self-harm when I was feeling especially bad or especially lonely.

The people I was surrounded with were mainly creative free spirits, so it was easy. There was no judgement. I had no regard for my body, so it didn't really matter what happened to it. It felt good when I knew I could seduce a man, or choose to accept his come-on or not, depending on my mood. I felt a sort of sexual power, a superficial confidence.

My sexuality confused me. I wanted sex – to connect, to see and be seen – and I didn't want it. I wanted men to want me and I wanted them to reject me. I wanted to be simultaneously fucked out of numbness and fucked into numbness.

All a man had to do was look at me in a certain way, and I recognised the darkness in him, and responded to it, matched it, sucked it up into me. This was a place for my trauma to go and be discharged, because any other way – drink or drugs, for example – would be out of my control. I had to control everything and, within that control, access the uncontrollable inside myself. My body was where my value both lay and from where it was discounted. Sometimes it felt dangerous to be inside myself, knowing how far and how easily I could take things.

I liked being a sexual person. On some level, I knew this was a good thing, to be connected to your sexuality and to feel free to express it. I don't think it was sex I always wanted, but to experience closeness with another human being, where it felt like the best of me lived, where my caring and generous parts could be expressed, where I could hold another person's vulnerability skilfully and safely. And mainly I wanted sex as a trade for the aftermath, for arms around me and a warm chest to put my head on and the feeling of being held, of being loved. Sometimes the man would just roll over, and I would be bereft. Sometimes I was the one who rolled over.

There were a couple of known predators in college. People joked about them. I joked about them too, shaking my head as if we were referring to a playful rogue instead of a sex offender. One night during first year, I was in a friend's apartment with some others. They were the cool guys, musicians and artists. We were drinking, and some people were smoking joints. As usual, I faded early, so I went into a bedroom and fell asleep.

Some time later, I was woken by a close friend, Nadine, clambering in next to me – I saw her face in the darkness, her eyes closed. Later, I woke up again. Nadine was gone and someone else was there. I could feel their presence, their weight. I looked around, bleary-eyed, and it was a boy from fourth year, P. I didn't really know him. He lived in the apartment we were in. He was friends with my fourth-year friends, one of the cool guys, and he dressed exactly like Bob Dylan.

He was trying to get on top of me and I stiffened. I heard a belt buckle and I swallowed and tried to turn over.

'What are you doing?' I whispered.

P sighed in apparent exasperation, and his penis was in my mouth then.

I didn't want it there. I hadn't said it could be there but it was happening, and I was drunk and so tired, and I was in his bed, and I was just a first year, and he was a fourth year, and everyone thought he was great, so it must be okay.

He took a blowjob from me. I froze and waited for it to be over. When he was finished, he immediately got up and left the room.

I tried to pretend that this was okay, that this was just like all the others. But I'd wanted all the others on some level. I was a drunk girl in a bed. P and I had never spoken, apart from saying hi to each other. He wasn't attracted to me. I didn't run away from him to my friends and tell them what he'd done. Why not? What is this paralysing thing that happens?

Compared to everything else that had gone on and was continuing to go on, it didn't seem like a big thing. I didn't recognise it as an assault. When you are used to abuse, assaults become part of the tapestry of your life.

The week after it happened I was in the Students' Union office, and P came in, leaned on the door and talked to the SU president while I was searching for something at the back of the room. I looked at him from this distance and considered him. He was wearing a cowboy hat. I thought, *Maybe I could make myself like him. Maybe I could force what happened into something else.*

P didn't speak to me for the rest of my time in college. Eventually, I found out he was a serial sex abuser, of first-year girls in particular. In 2005, there was no rape or sexual consent awareness in colleges. There was no support for victims or, at least, no explicit demonstration of support.

Four years later, I met P at a New Year's Eve dinner party and made sure he ended up sitting beside me. Deeply uncomfortable, he shuffled around and didn't make eye contact.

'It's good to see you again,' I said in a whisper. 'The last time I saw you, you had your dick in my mouth.'

A terrible but brilliant awkwardness draped over us.

'Mia, now is not the place,' he said, looking straight ahead.

As I considered my next move. My friend Manus, who knew what had happened, looked meaningfully at me from across the table, eyes of warning, of pleading, so I dropped it. The very second dinner was finished, P legged it.

I used to walk home from my job in a video shop through the small red-light district near my home. One night I was wrapped in my bright yellow coat with my earphones in. It was after 11 p.m., so I was walking fast. Men kerb-crawled all the time around the Benburb Street end of Stoneybatter. It was illegal, but they didn't care, and there were never any police checking anyway. Occasionally a car would slow down as it passed me, a shadow lowering inside as the man tried to get a look at me. I would keep walking, rigid and incensed. The women I saw down the side-streets floated like ghosts: rail thin, lank hair, they were not well. One time I was plodding home from work on a weekend afternoon, and a girl leaning against the bus shelter eyeballed me as I approached. I'd seen her that morning on my way to work.

'Is this your street?' she said.

'Sorry?'

'Is this your street?'

I looked blankly at her, trying to understand what she was asking.

'Doesn't matter,' she said quickly.

I felt exposed and weird. I thought about it on the way home. *Do I look like a prostitute? What do prostitutes look like? Does she know? Do people who have been exploited sense one another? Does she recognise something in me? Are all women potential prostitutes?* I suppose they are, simply because they're women. I had taken money from J and his friend for sexual acts, but I still hadn't connected any of it. I didn't consider myself to be a 'prostitute' because I hadn't had sex with them. I didn't like that I felt sorry for the girl, in her grey tracksuit, taking shelter in a bus stop. I didn't like how I pootled back to my normal middle-class life. My soft life, making art every day. While there she was, existing just down the road.

Another night I was coming home from work, and a carload of young lads shouted something at me. I was listening to my iPod and couldn't hear them properly. I thought they wanted directions. 'Sorry?' I said, my face fiercely friendly under my huge winter hat.

'How much?' they screamed again, howling, hanging out of the windows like hounds.

I have never been street smart, always gullible, always thinking people have good intentions. *How much is what?* The penny finally dropped and rage formed instantly. They had contempt for women, not only in the sex trade, but all women. What a laugh for them to drive around the streets abusing women. *How dare they?* I marched over to their car intent on ripping off the wipers, but the lights changed, and their pasty teenage faces filled with relieved laughter.

I raged all the way home. If this was how they treated a random woman walking home, how would they have behaved towards a woman involved in prostitution? I felt protective of every woman who hung around these streets, and I felt transparent, as if I was made of tracing paper.

When I was twenty-two, I got involved with an old friend, L. I needed love so badly and I couldn't just be normal about it. I pushed him away and simultaneously clung on to him, and he left after a few months. The more wholesome and 'pure' men were, the less I seemed to be capable of receiving their love. The more I wanted something, the more I rejected it.

After the break-up, I felt as if I had nothing left. When I was with L, I was able to absorb some of his goodness. After we broke up, I felt as if part of myself had been carved out of me. The night it happened, I stayed up vomiting late into the night.

A couple of weeks after this, forced Christmas joviality was in full swing and I was out with my friends from work having a terrible time. I walked home at about 3 a.m. It took a long time. I was drunk and upset. I rang and rang L. I was crying as I wobbled through the vomit-stained city-centre streets. I didn't care. I didn't try to wipe away my tears or look normal or get it together. Town was exploding around me, and no one noticed me anyway.

Two guys around my age, who were walking ahead, stopped when they heard me crying. They chatted with me. They were kind. I told them I had a broken heart. They tried to cheer me up and they walked me home. One seemed to disappear. I don't remember. I only remember bits. The other came into my house. He had a cup of tea and listened while I sat on the stairs and looked up at him with make-up splatted like paint on my face, trying to explain what had happened with my ex, how sad I was, how horrendous this feeling was, how much I hurt – it hurt too much to move or speak or think.

He told me his friend wasn't answering his phone. He didn't know where he was, he said. He was lost. He'd have to stay if that was okay with me. He had no way of getting home. I didn't care how drunk I was or how upset I was. I didn't care how I looked. I didn't care about anything. I just wanted all my feelings to stop.

I didn't think he'd find anything about me attractive, considering my condition. I didn't think he'd hurt me. I wasn't able to stop it happening. It was violent and mean. I was nothing. I had no words. I was scooped out. I wasn't there. I was limbless, lifeless, zoned straight out of my body and out of my mind. I remember he called me a bitch. I remember getting sick. I got sick on him. He didn't stop. He didn't care. He kept his hands on me, keeping me where I was. I remember gagging. It wasn't consensual sex. And it was consensual because he was an implement I was using to hurt myself.

But what I did or did not do was irrelevant because it happened around me, like how the air temperature changes.

I woke up and saw the back of this man's head next to me. I closed my eyes and pretended it was my ex-boyfriend. I cuddled up to him, still pretending. I wrapped an arm around him. He was tall and skinny, not like my ex at all, who had a much stockier, softer frame. I forced him to mutate into my former love. *I can get used to this new body*, I thought, this reincarnation of my ex. It had happened, so I had to make it be okay, like how children jam jigsaw pieces into the wrong spaces. A cut on his shoulder had bled onto the sheets during the night. When I saw the dried blood, I jumped, thinking it was mine, expecting it to be.

Consent and boundaries coexist; one brings life to the other. If you feel a boundary being pushed, you have the choice to hold it up. I did not have this skill; I did not have this awareness. I was wordless. I had no language when I felt something was wrong. Boundary violation had a numbing effect on me. When we have been traumatised, we can react with fight, flight, freeze or fawn. Our bodies choose the safest option. Fight and flight have never been available to me. I always freeze or fawn.

During my early twenties, I experienced a lot of pseudo-rape: you fall asleep in a friend's house and wake up to find someone pushing themselves against you. You say, 'No, thanks', but he keeps nagging and nagging until you give in. Or when a cuddle turns into touching and, even though you tell him no with your body language, you curl your spine towards him, he keeps finding ways in and around your resistance. Many women can relate to what I'm describing, but don't talk about it because it's not rape: they agreed to it, they 'consented', but it isn't willing sex.

Being a participant in your own violation brings a dense kind of shame. And it feels the same as rape because in a sense it *is* rape. It feels violating and wrong because it is. And you're left with a sense of grubbiness and unease about having given in. But then you don't want to speak about your experience because it wasn't *rape*-rape, was it? Not in the legal definition. So maybe you've no right to these feelings of violation. Let me tell you, it may not fit the legal definition of rape, but it fits the moral one. You have every right to your feelings, every right to express them, and you've every right to feel rage at the man who ignored your boundaries and used your body for his sexual gratification.

When your boundaries have been eroded so slowly that you're not even fully aware of it happening, it can be difficult to reclaim them. It's hard to know what a boundary feels like.

It can be hard for a young woman to maintain sexual boundaries, when the societal message is that their value lies in how fuckable they are. I think a lot of men are aware of this. I think predators can sense vulnerability, like wolves can smell blood. Men who are not so inclined cannot understand it, and don't necessarily experience it, so they cannot relate to women when we tell our stories. I'm not sure that even the most compassionate and understanding men will ever get it.

Each time a man treated me with disrespect, I was convinced I was this sexual thing. I was not convinced of the failings of men, only of my own failings as a woman. Some of my friends said they never got cat-called. Others said they enjoyed it or thought it was funny, so they shrugged it off. I was irritated that they couldn't see the explicit misogyny. But I cared so much because my value of myself was based on how others received me: if I was treated as a sexual object, then that made me a sexual object. I wondered if I was making up my feelings, if I needed to relax a bit.

Everything was normal. I was making video projects involving clowns. I played the clown. I had days of panicking over an unfinished project, staring at a clump of metal as Brendan the technician told me, 'You have to give everything three times longer than you think', and, the next day, I'd be drinking, taking drugs and having sex, and then I'd be wondering if the new boy I'd met liked me or not.

Life was full and confusing and vibrant, and I was not concerned with politics or the state of the world or feminism or rape or abuse. Everything was short term. I was twenty-one and the many friendships I had were easy. I mostly liked who I was. I felt free, and nothing was serious or that hard yet.

Late one night, I was walking up my street on the way home from the city centre, and a small chubby man was bustling along behind me. He started to chat with me, and that was fine. I was wearing an olive green skirt and a yellow belt. I can remember the skirt's thin fabric, its pattern, how it felt around me.

The man was twice my age, in his forties. We got to my

house. I don't remember how it happened, but he came in for a cup of tea and I gave him oral sex. If he'd had any contraception, I know I would have let him have sex with me. I didn't know why I was doing this. I didn't know that everything that had gone before made it inevitable. All I knew was that my power evaporated when men wanted something from me. I became passive, mute and available. I flopped and played possum. It was as if a dress had been laid out for me that perfectly fitted every curve and corner of my body and personality. Like I was made for it. The man was funny and friendly, in *awe* of me, in *awe* of what was happening, and I liked it. It felt great to provide this friendly little man with an unexpected surprise. It felt great to be so open and generous.

He asked for my phone number, and I gave it to him, and also told him I was an escort. The words spilled out of my mouth as if they had been waiting to be released, like I was acting in a film. This was my role, and it felt right. That was my job now. Not being me, but being *this*. Making people happy made me feel so good about myself. I made them feel better about themselves. The man said he wasn't into 'paying for it', and I felt at once relieved and insulted. But it wasn't enough. I wanted again to hold my worth in my hands and know it was real.

In her heart she is a mourner for those who have
not survived. In her soul she is a warrior for those
who are now as she was then. In her life she is both a
celebrant and proof of women's capacity and will
to survive, to become, to act, to change self and society.
And each year she is stronger and there are more of her.

Andrea Dworkin, *Letters from a War Zone*

COMFORT WOMEN

She is rated out of five stars.

Her body parts are commented on.

What she selects to show of her personality is assessed.

What she is unable to hide of herself is assessed.

The shape of her breasts, stomach, thighs is commented on.

Whether she looks her age or not is commented on.

They comment on her willingness to endure anal sex.

They complain about the lack thereof.

They write what it was like for them to have sex with her.

In their eyes, she is a piece of merchandise. She is a piece of meat.

I used a couple of different sex-trade websites to advertise on, and I used different names for each one. On these websites, men can find hundreds of women all over Ireland selling sexual 'services'. There is at least one in every town. One of the biggest escort websites has been run by a convicted pimp and former RUC officer Peter McCormick, and his business partner Audrey Campbell. In 2010, McCormick's son Mark was convicted of running brothels. Trafficked women connected to a Romanian gang have been advertised on these sites. The women had tattoos of barcodes. The websites call themselves 'online directories'.

You can pick your escort from the menu: look at her photos, read her reviews, call her and make an appointment after work. You can shop for her, the same as you shop online for anything else. It may or may not be the same 'girl' you 'admired' in the photos, but if you're turned on and expecting sex, any female body will do.

Men of all ages connect on forums in an online community. They approach 'punting' as if it's a hobby. Sometimes they refer to themselves as 'hobbyists'. Sometimes they refer to the women they pay to have sex with as 'service providers'. They discuss: 'Who is the best at anal right now?' and 'Good oral in Kildare.' It's an online support group for the sick at heart, everyone validating each other's sickness.

Our need to connect with others who share our values and beliefs is written into our DNA. Without others to share your beliefs and values, you can feel very lonely and isolated. These websites normalise the behaviour that the punters cannot share with anyone else in their life. It's okay when everyone else is doing it, after all.

This online culture helped me to feel that what I was

doing was okay too. When we do not have a solid sense of self, it is so much easier to attach ourselves to people and values we don't necessarily know are good or bad for us. I look back on my younger self – my accepting, non-judgemental, open way of being – and feel I need to protect her, wrap her in cotton wool and cover it with barbed wire.

At any one time, between eight hundred and a thousand women are advertised for sex on escort sites in Ireland. This does not include the 'sugar dating' phenomenon and social media. An estimated one in fifteen Irish men pay for sexual access, meaning there may be more than a hundred thousand 'punters' in Ireland, compared to about a thousand female 'service providers'. Why are we not talking about these men? Why are *they* not talking? In the debates about prostitution, we do not hear from them. They don't 'come out'. They don't create associations or campaign for 'punters' rights'. If punting is the legitimate and harmless hobby they claim it to be, why not?

There is a lot of money to be made from operating brothels and running an escort website. Advertising is very expensive – one 'online directory' of women in prostitution had a turnover of six million euro in 2015. The men pay around a hundred euro for thirty minutes of sex with a woman, around two hundred for an hour. And with more than a hundred thousand punters, there is obviously no shortage of male demand for women's bodies. We know that most women in the sex trade are not there voluntarily, and when we understand the concept that sexual consent has to be freely given, voluntary and reversible, it is inarguable that when people defend the sex trade in Ireland, they are defending the daily rape of women and girls. The pimps who run the websites become multimillionaires by serving up a literal rape market.

The first part of acknowledging a reality is naming it as one. Language can be a balm to the unspeakable truth. We use 'child abuse' instead of 'child rape'. In recent years, the palatable term 'non-consensual sex' has appeared to describe rape. Instead of naming the agents of male harm – men – we say 'violence against women' and 'gender-based violence', leaving out the perpetrator and treating these crimes as though they are unfortunate and inevitable storms that magically appear out of nowhere and in the face of which we are helpless.

Mentioning the word 'male' or 'men's' before 'violence' is a radical act for which you will receive total silence, a tense atmosphere or the inevitable backlash of 'not all men'. We talk about how many women have been raped instead of how many men have raped. We talk about 'abusive relationships' when a relationship has no ability to abuse, only a participant in it. Headlines speak of increases in 'domestic violence' instead of increases in male violence against women. The only person to be seen in these language structures is the woman, so therefore our awareness lands on her instead of on the agent of harm.

The Japanese once referred to Chinese, Korean and Filipino sex slaves as 'comfort women' – the reality of male brutality towards women erased for the sake of psychological comfort. Language has the power to change a culture, and those who profit from the exploitation of women want to have the culture on their side, which helps them to operate with impunity.

When prostitution is established as legitimate 'work', and punters, therefore, as legitimate 'clients', there is no need for any critique. Getting us there means using terms like 'sex work', 'sex worker', 'survival sex worker', 'youth sex worker', 'child sex worker' and 'migrant sex worker'. Reassuring, cushioning, disguising language. We use language and words that morph what is going on into something else. We don't say 'prostitution'. We like to think that prostitution is what happens on the crude streets, shoved full of addiction and desperation, separate from 'real, high-end sex work'. The policing of such language stops those of us who might have questions, for fear of saying the wrong thing or offending someone or doing feminism 'wrong'. It comforts some and lets others off the hook.

Prostitution is routinely defended as 'the oldest profession', which will 'never go away' and therefore should be accepted. This claim is inaccurate, avoidant and defeatist. Slavery is also ancient, yet we don't accept it. Rape, child sexual abuse and poverty will also never 'go away', yet we hear nobody calling for these horrors to be accepted as a tolerable part of our society.

Sex-trade advocates compare 'work' in the sex trade to working in McDonald's or cleaning toilets, jobs that earn a minimum hourly wage. They don't talk about why 'visiting' an escort costs two hundred euro per hour. They say that if it's forced, it isn't 'sex work', but they call the women 'survival sex workers' anyway, as if being forced by poverty is any different from being forced by a pimp. It's 'Sex work is work' and 'My body my choice', but don't think about those who have no choice about what happens to their body as they are transported around Ireland to sexually serve the hundred thousand Irish men. And as long as we're all distracted, arguing over whether prostitution is 'work', we're not thinking about the choices of those men who pay to rape vulnerable women, and the men running the sex trade who profit from it. They can sit back and laugh at the Twitter debates and think-pieces on Medium.com.

A levels or A means anal sex.
Bareback means no-condom sex.

CIM means 'come in mouth'.

COB means 'come on body.'

Covered means wearing a condom.

Facial means 'come on face'.

GFE means 'girlfriend experience'.

OWO means oral without a condom.

PSE means porn-star experience.

Uncovered means no condom.

The men leave reviews of the women they pay to have sex with and rate them out of five stars in various categories: *accuracy of photos, location, satisfaction, physical appearance, value for money, overall experience*. They note whether they would recommend the woman or not, and if they would repeat the experience. Most men do not repeat because they want variety.

When we're talking about sex, we're talking about subjectivity so intricate and complex that it is beyond evaluation. Sexuality is an instinct, an expression, not a skill. Being reviewed on sex is like being reviewed on how you respond to art, music or wine preferences. It is unfair and nonsensical, and it denies our humanity. There exists no 'rent a friend' scheme for lonely people because, in a relationship, we understand mutuality and that, if it is paid for, it cannot be authentic, so it isn't an actual friendship. So what changes when it's a sexual relationship?

Reviews clearly show us that men pay women for sex so they don't have to deal with them as full human beings, with sexual preferences, thoughts and feelings, or take into account what they are experiencing. They also pay women to consent to sex so they don't have to acknowledge their own personal failings or inadequacies, which being rejected by a woman might reveal to them. The review system is toxic masculinity on steroids, but somehow, conveniently for the men, stays out of the gaze of mainstream feminism.

In some reviews, the men splurge with indulgent and vacuous flattery. They make bad private jokes. They add winking emojis, as though they share some sort of cute secret with the women, as though the whole thing isn't the mortifying charade it is. As consumers, they are free to criticise a woman and how she has responded sexually. The men stamp their feet because they didn't get oral sex without a condom. They complain that someone was outside the room the entire time; they heard a knock when the time was up; they heard male voices coming from another room. They complain that she had a saggy tummy or that she was older than she said in her ad or that her excuse not to have anal sex wasn't genuine. Over and over, they say that she had 'not a word of English' and 'she wasn't the girl in the pictures'. Rather than this being what it is – a blatant sign of sex trafficking – it is simply something to be complained about in their precious wankfest of an online support group. Do you think the men who write these reviews call the police or the dedicated sex-trafficking hotline? Of course they don't.

Punters write that there was a lack of 'chemistry' or 'connection' as though this was something the woman was supposed to be able to magically invent or fake. They mostly complain that she seemed 'unwilling', that she was 'lazy', that she was mechanical or that the sex 'felt mechanical'. One punter's review reads, 'Totally useless, crap at her job.'

They want the woman to be a sexual machine and do everything asked of her without refusal or complaint, but they also want her to fake that she's not a sexual machine. She must look happy doing it. She can express feelings, but only the male-pleasing ones. One articulate man on the punter support group forum wrote, 'I must get the impression that my pleasure is important to her – and that she isn't just trying to get through the appointment. The reality may be quite different, but the impression she gives me is what counts.' These men understand perfectly well what they are doing.

The men who describe a woman as 'mechanical' are clearly aware that something is awry with her. When we are in the 'freeze' response, we dissociate and act mechanically, robotically. Freeze and dissociation are trauma responses. The men are knowingly having sex with traumatised women, but they don't care because they have paid not to care. Advocates say it is 'her body, her choice', except that paying for sex is quite literally the man paying her so that he can do what *he* wants with her body.

It comes down to this: if men believed that sex was a mutual activity between two human beings based on equal respect and power, the sex trade would not exist.

In one study it was unsurprisingly found that men who pay for sexual access are statistically far more likely to be rapists than those who don't. Paying for a woman to sexually acquiesce is just another way of getting around authentic mutual consent. What else do we call sexual intercourse when the sexual pleasure and agency are one-sided? Or where the sex is on one person's terms? Or where the woman's body freezes and dissociates to endure it? What's another word for unwanted sex?

In paid-for sex, women are products and men are consumers. Women are objects and men are users. Men who pay for sexual access are inherently sexual predators, because when sexual 'consent' is purchased, the very concept of it is rendered void. This truth doesn't change if the man is not fully aware that he is a predator. And while a punter most likely does not see himself as a rapist, his mind might be extremely concentrated on this aspect of himself if he was to discover his own twenty-one-year-old daughter waiting on the bed, instead of another young woman. Sourced from the same misogynistic pool of narcissistic, sexual entitlement to a woman's body, punters and rapists blend together as one.

Prostitution is the ideal environment for these men to express power and control because, in our society, it is normalised, ignored or shrugged off with jokes. In any other context, it is seen for what it is – violation. I haven't seen this attitude in relation to male landlords attempting to exploit the housing crisis by offering female tenants rent-free accommodation in exchange for weekly sex. We all understand this as exploitative. But, for many, it appears that it is acceptable for a certain cohort of women to be targeted by predators, as long as they are financially compensated. This lack of critical analysis gives a free pass to punters who feel validated in their exertion of power and control, which gives them an orgasmic thrill in the meeting, which they can then repeat when they get home and write a review.

I was seduced by temporarily feeling valued and further groomed by the culture surrounding it; the constant messaging that my value lay in my sexual appeal to men. I called the punters 'clients' and charged for my time. There was no problem. I needed it to be okay. *Why shouldn't men pay me for sex? Why shouldn't I sell it? It's my body. I can do what I want, as long as I don't tell anyone. And I'm proud of myself for being tough enough to do this.* A punter could have done anything to me and I would have endured it. I was proud of this trait – the secret, embedded trait of the used and abused.

I thought the punters and I were on the same team, as long as everyone abided by the unspoken rules and kept up the façade. I could survive psychologically, as long as I didn't have to think too deeply about what I was doing. I liked punters, and I didn't like them. I didn't judge them. I had tender or funny moments with many of them. I found them threatening, and I found them safe. I found the ease with which they produced and swallowed lies pathetic. I hated them for deceiving their wives. I liked making them feel at ease. I hated feeling like a masturbatory tool. I liked feeling useful.

I heard an interview on RTÉ radio with an African woman who was trafficked to Ireland and kept for two years in a house in the west of Ireland. Eventually, she managed to steal a key and escape. She came across someone in the street and the first thing she said to them was 'What country am I in?' Two years is more than seven hundred days of multiple rapes. She said that at least eighty per cent of the men who paid to use her body were Irish. These are men we know, who are in our families, groups and communities. What happened to them that they would pay to use the body of a slave for the sake of an orgasm?

Owing to the acceptance of men 'paying for sex', to our jaded acceptance of women as sexual subordinates to men, to the proliferation of violent and misogynistic pornography, and so much more, this woman's case did not cause a national uproar. It did not cause the response that sexual slavery occurring in our country should have done.

We are appalled at the international stories of girls and young women being kidnapped by 'monsters' and kept in bunkers as these men's personal sexual slaves. Yet when it involves money, and no easily identifiable 'monster', we don't care so much. Why are we, as a nation, not boiling with fury over Irish men paying to rape vulnerable foreign women every day? How bad does it have to get before we will, and what is the cost in the meantime?

These websites on which trafficking victims are advertised operate from foreign jurisdictions, which means they get around the Irish law forbidding the solicitation of sexual services. There seems little point in it being illegal to pay for sexual access while it remains legal for pimps to advertise it.

You don't need to be on a prostitution website to sell sex – you don't even need to advertise yourself. The men will find you one way or another. Anywhere a woman is vulnerable, whether that is psychologically, circumstantially or otherwise, male sexual predators will prey on her. There have been reports that vulnerable female residents in direct-provision centres are being targeted for prostitution. They experience local men driving up beside them and soliciting them, or men who ask male residents to act as go-betweens.

When the woman says no, she is coerced with responses like: 'Don't you want to support your family?' When we regard prostitution as 'work', we reframe attempts to coerce women to have sex into someone offering a job opportunity. We diminish a woman's sense of indignity and violation. It's just a job. Simply say no and continue to live on nineteen euro a week if you don't want to do it.

You don't need to be as vulnerable as a woman in direct provision for the tendrils of sexual exploitation to surround you. Men seek vulnerability on social-media accounts and through dating apps. Anywhere there is vulnerability, there are predators. I've recently heard about porn recruiters using a popular dating app to look for young women specifically aged between eighteen and twenty-two.

A few years ago, I registered on a 'Sugar Baby' site, posing as a twenty-three-year-old student called Emma. The websites are vague, describing 'mutually beneficial relationships' and 'arrangements', instead of calling it what it is: older men paying to fuck women young enough to be their daughters, paying them to mould their personality to fit the man's desires. There is already a power differential in a relationship between an older man and a much younger woman; adding money to it exploits that power differential.

The language is insipid and innocent-sounding – 'sugar

baby', 'sugar daddy' – designed to groom us into a false sense of legitimacy. It even has its own verb – 'sugaring'. The ambiguity surrounding 'sugaring', and the messaging that it is akin to 'dating', means that the level of stigma is not nearly as high as being a 'sex worker'. There are many sugar-baby websites, and thousands more young women are involved than those explicitly advertising on escort websites.

Before my photo was approved, I was sent dozens of messages by middle-aged men asking me for 'car meets' and 'two-hour meets' in hotel rooms, messages that started, 'Are you around tonight?'

There were messages from men offering me a hundred and fifty euro for sex, three hundred euro for sex. When I told one man that a hundred and fifty was too little, he offered to double it. He said he was 'quite fun, so you might even waive the fee'.

Other openers asked me if I was 'a kinky girl who likes anal', if I was submissive, if I would allow myself to be tied up. One man asked me if I wanted to meet up for 'fun' and when I asked what 'fun', he replied, 'NSA [no strings attached] sex every now and then.' Another man said, 'I need total discretion. One-hour hotel meet, nothing weird, all consensual, gift three hundred and fifty euro.' A fifty-five-year-old man who thought he was communicating with a twenty-three-year-old woman said he'd give me 'a cash pressie' every time we had sex. One man, out of about fifteen, asked me to go for coffee with him rather than soliciting me for paid sex. The men asked me repeatedly to send them a photo of myself on the app 'Kik', which I hadn't heard of. Kik, it turns out, is an anonymous messaging app for sending pictures without sharing phone numbers. When they said 'photo', they meant one of my naked body.

Thousands of eighteen- to twenty-five-year-old women are on these sugar-dating sites because they need money – to survive, for validation, for self-esteem, to re-enact trauma, who knows? What matters is that they are there and that there are too many men willing to exploit them.

When eleven Limerick men were convicted of soliciting for sex in 2012, the *Limerick Leader* refused to publish their names. Social media was full of apologists. *Why mortify them more than they already have been? Why embarrass them by revealing their names? What if they have a loveless marriage? Why destroy their families?* The stretching to accommodate this behaviour was outrageous.

The questions that should have been asked were: *What is it about the crimes these men committed that makes them exempt from the usual journalistic protocol? Why is it still acceptable to protect men's dignity at the expense of women and girls being raped? Where is the compassion for the poor pimped foreign women they paid their way inside? Where is the sympathy for the wives, partners and families of these men? Why do men with teenage daughters pay Romanian girls to give them blowjobs during their lunch break?*

Why are we so forgiving and understanding of the men who pay for sexual access and so judgemental of those who sell it? Maybe it's for the same reason that we excuse and justify the actions of rapists and other sexual offenders, and disbelieve or discredit their victims or minimise their experience. By doing so, we don't have to acknowledge that the man really chose to do that – that everyday evil is a real thing. If we can make it so the man's behaviour is somehow the woman's responsibility, even in a small way, we can turn away from her pain and get on with our lives. We can avoid the consequent feelings of discomfort, and the responsibility that we could do something about it. This cognitive bias is framed by the backdrop of an unequal, patriarchal society, which is often expressed in insidious, slanted ways in our beliefs and attitudes towards men and women. It isn't our fault, but once we are aware of it, it is our responsibility to turn towards rather than away.

The world in which women and girls exist is a world in which they cannot win, in which their only option is to take the crumbs that fall off the table of power, settle for them and somehow make them work The patriarchy is about men having power over women, and the ultimate subjugation of a woman is sexual domination – this is where she is broken.

Cultural messaging has conditioned women and girls to expect and welcome objectification and male entitlement to their bodies, to endure pain, and to celebrate the performance of that endurance, gaslighting us so we think we are simultaneously the source of the problem and also its solution. I do not wish that women had a equal standing in a patriarchal world. I wish for them to be liberated from it.

I know how inviting it can feel to accept and internalise this inequality. It is no wonder that so many young women cling to the status quo, try to make a comfortable home for themselves within the patriarchy, engage in conduct that invites validation, instead of rejection. It is no wonder they enter sugar babying, prostitution and pornography, or objectify themselves on social-media platforms and sell their X-rated content online. It is no wonder there are videos on social media of very young women being punched in the face or choked by men, and smiling into the camera afterwards. They share it and get validation from others celebrating their entrepreneurial spirit, their empowerment, their 'kink'.

Choking during sex, which has been the subject of several recent murder inquiries, has become a heterosexual sex 'trend'. Naturally, the women are the ones being choked by men, and nobody questions this ancient expression of male power. In a desperate bid to internalise and make this uptick in violent male behaviour acceptable, magazine articles, memes and Twitter threads appeared with instructions to men on how to do it 'safely'.

When we see one thread of the tapestry of misogyny, we can't unsee it. It is easier to pretend we don't see it than have to confront the fact that the material our world is draped in is poisonous.

It can't all be oppressive all the time. We have to survive in the water in which we swim. We have to make things be reasonable and okay for us to experience. We have to have spaces where we don't feel as if we're drowning, or we would lose our minds.

We're sold this warped picture of what 'liberation' for women is supposed to mean, what equality is supposed to mean, by apparently subverting the male gaze by using it for our own 'gain'. But we're all being groomed without realising it. It seems to me that, although there has been some progress towards women's equity, we are going backwards when it comes to women's sexuality. The backlash against feminism is bigger than I've ever seen it – with Men Going Their Own Way groups, Men's Rights Activists, 'involuntary celibate' terrorist groups and a porn-saturated online culture, where young women selling sexual pictures of themselves is seen as empowering rather than feeding male sexual entitlement to female bodies. Young women and girls are being conditioned to absorb their own dehumanisation into their sexuality and we are celebrating it. Repressing and objectifying women's sexuality are two sides of the same coin of oppression. Either way, women's sexuality is in the hands of men.

Imagine there is a rotting tree in the middle of a park. It needs to be removed. Instead, a bunch of people arrive and make it look better. They prune its branches and clean up its bark so that it looks like any other tree in the park. Nobody complains about it anymore, but the tree continues rotting into the ground beneath it. That tree is our patriarchal society. Liberal feminism means very well and does a lot of good work in removing much of the tree in the pruning, but it is so accepting of the tree's existence that it thinks patching things up and reframing something rotten as healthy will improve the situation for everyone who has to experience the tree.

Liberal feminism does not want to concern itself with the dark and mangled roots polluting the soil. People compliment the tree on how beautiful it is and forget that it is rotting inside.

A second group of people come along and hack the tree out of the ground with axes. It is a lot of work and takes a very long time. There is much noise and disruption in the park. Nobody is happy. People have to change their dog-walking routes and can't stop at their usual benches. The attractive tree they liked looking at is gone. A big ugly hole remains. The park-goers give out to the second group of people for causing all this. This group is radical feminism. Petitions are sent to the council. Protests take place. People shout things like 'Give us back our tree!' Radical feminism knows that not only is it possible to cut the tree out of the ground, it is also possible to grow something different in its place. It is not popular, but it is getting to the root of the problem instead of pruning its branches.

Much pro-sex-trade advocacy is around a woman's choice to do what she wants with her body. This is claimed to be a feminist perspective. The thing about feminism, though, is that it isn't about individuality. Feminism is a social and political movement to liberate all women from systems of male oppression. I believe that our personal choices can be political, but if our politics remains in the realm of personal choice, then our ability to see the bigger picture and create lasting change for all women is limited. As a feminist, my personal experience of equity is irrelevant as long as women are being driven around the country for Irish men to exploit sexually. It is irrelevant as long as abusive men continue to receive suspended sentences for beating up their partners and as long as men continue to rape women. It is irrelevant because I could as easily be living the lives of those women as I am living my own.

When women participate in unequal systems like prostitution, we can defend the systems with greater ease. 'There's a girl on Twitter who says she loves her job,' we tell ourselves. 'She seems fine. It's *her* body.' So the critique of the system stops there, at the level of individuality. We try not to look, not to see. We ignore the issue that men are paying for women to sexually serve them; we ignore the evidence from studies that demonstrate the harrowing psychological impact of prostitution on women and girls; we ignore the bigger picture of sexism and inequality. We don't want to do anything that would recall the not-so-historic Ireland that brutalised women and girls for having a sexuality. If they choose it, it must be okay, we reason.

Arguing that women have the right to sell sex disguises another argument: that men have the right to buy it. This is a rarely, if ever, spoken of aspect of the sex trade, which is remarkable considering that men paying for sexual access is the sole reason it exists.

Technology pushes us ever forwards, and sexist systems adapt to take on new guises. We think things are different because a young woman selling explicit content on 'Onlyfans' is not controlled by a pimp. She is in charge of her own objectification, and this is reframed as progress. A few, select women earn a lot of money and we think how empowering it must be. We gasp and feel a thrill at the concept of a small crumb of power. I am reminded of something I read a long time ago, along the lines of it being much more comfortable to carry your own lead than be led by someone else. But, either way, you are wearing a lead.

In years to come, there will be many traumatised young women who simply did what cultural messaging told them was empowering and feminist, who internalised their choices into an identity they held on to tightly, even as they were being harmed.

Sex-trade advocates dismiss the question, 'Would you want your daughter selling sex?' with deflections such as, 'I wouldn't want my daughter working as a paramedic either' or they say that the question isn't relevant, only the 'working conditions'. However, the subjective question about our daughters is highly relevant: it brings the reality home to us, and our gut response reveals to us all we need to know. It is telling that the advocates prefer to deflect it; either we want the best life possible for our daughters or we are sociopathic.

I've seen what happens to women who speak about their experiences of sexual violence, particularly commercial sexual exploitation. I've seen the online abuse, the level of cruelty that is staggering to behold. I've seen the doxing, the threats, the attempts to shut the person up out of fear, the fake websites, the fake pictures, the doctored documents, the petitions, the protests, the book-launch stormings, the attempts to 'cancel', the blatant lies, and the vitriol spewing from social-media accounts – both anonymous and identified – to the victims of male violence.

When you have received money to endure that violence you are magically not a victim any more. Remember, 'You weren't complaining when you were raking it in.' Obviously social media – which can and does perpetrate 'real-life' damage – is no place for a nuanced and understanding discussion of something as complex as the sex trade, but this awareness doesn't lessen the impact of experiencing it directed at you. It concerns me that too few of us are willing to expand our awareness outside what we read online, something that is particularly in relation to digital natives – those who have been raised with the internet.

I want girls to be free of any chance of involvement in the sex trade as they grow up. I do not care if that means the women who are involved by 'choice' – and who have the privilege of picking and choosing the punters, who can take time off and need not accept punters out of desperation – will have to find another job. I want the entire thing shut down. The game is fixed for us to lose. This stuff is not a reclaiming of anything. It is feeding the system. The sex trade is a very old, very obvious patriarchal structure, set up by men for men. It is therefore not feminist to perpetuate the patriarchal structure, regardless of your own individual circumstances. Feminism is about serving women as a class. It is about the world we want our daughters to inherit.

Cash is evidence of coercion *and* evidence of 'consent' in the sex trade. And monetary compensation eradicates feelings and the ability to ask questions because we like to think things are one way or another: choice or abuse. This is true for the women involved (I got paid for it, didn't I?) and for the men (I paid her, didn't I?). When choice and abuse coexist, we struggle to sift through the nuance: it is too dark and hard to think about. But people 'choose' to hurt themselves in myriad ways that we recognise as harmful – women defending an abusive partner, alcohol and drug misuse, self-harm marks on a wrist, smoking. We understand these things to be harmful while holding compassion for the individuals involved. We have to do the same thing with the sex trade. Women are being traumatised by men and we are calling it 'work', potentially making prostitution the most insidious form of sexual abuse because it is not recognised as sexual abuse. It is okay to campaign against the pay gap and against sexist jokes in the workplace and against street harassment, but prostitution and pornography speak to something far darker within masculinity and, when we raise it, we are reminded, as we have been for centuries, to shut up, by both men and women alike.

Advocating the existence of the sex trade or pornography is not doing anything radical or new or feminist. Feminism is supposed to cause ruffles in male entitlement and value systems, not soothe them. Paying for sexual gratification is illegal, and people who continue to advocate 'choice' and who argue that 'sex work is work' are merely accommodating male comfort and letting them off the hook for brutalising women. They are erasing the mental and physical trauma most of these women will carry secretly for the rest of their lives, unable to name or speak openly about because society would rather see it simply as a job they were stupid enough to do.

In the sex trade and porn wars, it is tempting to label and vilify those on 'the other side'. I invite us to be curious about the stark discrepancy between views and conclusions, and to be open to discovering what the space between reveals. I imagine it has less to do with the actual truth and more to do with the complexity of being human; our attachments, our insecurities, our egos.

There is no shame in surviving, and there is no shame in being a young woman trying to navigate and negotiate this unfair, sexist, misogynistic world, but shame on any culture that promotes the commodification of female sexuality to young girls as something progressive, and on the complicit male adults, who definitely know better.

Because sexist attitudes have been ingrained in our culture for centuries, I cannot imagine what a world without them would look like. I close my eyes and see nothingness, a place razed to the ground. Some day, when I am long dead, our successors will look back with horror that the sex trade, strip clubs and pornography ever existed, that we once treated women in that way, just as we look back on the recent history of rape being legal within marriage, of the Magdalene Laundries, of the marriage bar, of women not being allowed to vote or pursue an education. There will be museums, and people will shake their heads in dismay.

I want to imagine that world. I imagine how safe women would feel, how they could trust the world a little bit more. I imagine how therapeutic it would be for women to feel a sense of justice, to know that our history of oppression is explicitly condemned. A world where girls grow up to discover their sexuality on their own terms, not from how pornography depicts them or from how porn-infused boys treat them.

Sexualities develop naturally, in their own time and in their own way, with moments of connection and exploration. I imagine a world where women feel the right to safety in their bones, where women's suffering at the hands of men is not taken as an unfortunate, tragic, unpreventable norm. In this world, misogyny doesn't get a chance to develop: women are respected sexually and in every way. Women are released from the stranglehold of needing to be likeable and easy-going and not 'too much' because no such messaging to mute or contain ourselves exists. Women do not resign themselves to unnecessary pain, humiliation and competition with other women for the resources over which men hold power. Women are trusted and believed in relation to their medical issues. Their pain is no longer discounted or sidelined. Angry and loud women are accepted without judgement. They are allowed to be wholly themselves. Girls don't get raped, cat-called or groomed. If there is a sexual predator or murderer at large, women won't be told not to walk alone after dark. Instead, men will be given a curfew and will accept this with understanding. Men don't review women on sex-trade websites because sex-trade websites don't exist. I know that this world is idealistic, and maybe I am naive to try to imagine it. And I can't imagine it, but I know that the air there is clean. I imagine myself breathing in this clean air.

The only legend I have ever loved
is the story of a daughter lost in hell.
And found and rescued there.

Eavan Boland, 'The Pomegranate'

BERLIN

After college, I moved to Berlin. One of my older sisters lives there and, every time I visited her, I noticed that I felt a real sense of freedom in being myself. From my experience, the people in Berlin don't really care very much about what you do or what you're like. They just seem to take you as you are.

I think this was a transitional time between one world and another, one version of myself melting into another; my thawing-out period. My only concern was myself. Despite the limitations of trying to earn money and not having my friends around, I felt like I belonged, and I have not found a better sensation yet, or a greater sense of freedom, than cycling through Berlin's streets. I was not yet preoccupied with social issues, or what had happened to me, or how I could contribute to making a safer society for women. I was twenty-five and my life was just about me.

I saw my sister a lot, took her kids to the playground and inhaled the clear, autumn air while they played. We went to flea markets, ate *Apfeltaschen* and drank coffee. I taught English as a foreign language and was good at it. I liked being centred on other people, being helpful, and the performance of it. I made art. I worked at an international art fair and did what transpired to be an ill-advised art internship. I made some friends. I saw a lot of theatre. I bought cheap furniture and moved into a ground-floor apartment with a couple, their elderly Rottweiler and two cats. The apartment was in a courtyard with trees growing in it. Every morning, I would wake up and the sunlight would be pouring in between the curtains onto my walls and sheets. Everything was a novelty. Even shopping for food was a novelty. Cycling anywhere was a novelty.

I discovered the English Theatre Berlin, and a theatre company I worked with to design and build sets. On my first visit to the theatre studio, I cycled through the entrance leading to the courtyard, and a boy cycled by me in the other direction, and I looked at him. He could have been coming from any of the offices, but I knew that I would get to know him and that it would be a significant knowing. At the next theatre company meeting, there he was: the stage manager's assistant, from Dublin, like me.

S was my friend first, for a couple of months. He had his own vulnerabilities, fragilities and awkwardness, but he seemed to accept himself, which I found intriguing. I liked being around him. I knew I just had to wait and he would come to me eventually. We hung around the edges of our feelings until an abnormally balmy November night in an empty playground when he kissed me. It meant so much to me that I cannot put it into words. I cannot fit words around how much I needed the gentleness, the softness, the way he held me, the care. He didn't try to have sex with me that night, and I was relieved, a quiet pressure gone. There was no performance. I was okay. It was safe.

We held hands, we went for walks and cycled around Berlin. We played a lot of outdoor table tennis. I used to hit the ball into the undergrowth on purpose, so he would have to go looking for it, and then I'd hide and wait breathless behind a tree while he was forced to look for me. It was like being a child. I was having so much fun.

Sex was fun too, the freeness and easiness of it. He unwrapped me, or a part of me. It felt a little like my first relationship at seventeen, the same sense of safety, of being seen whole and loved for it. What a new concept to get my head around – he was kind but that didn't mean that I owed him anything. I trusted myself to trust him and experienced what it was like to have sex in an equal capacity, the power equally shared. Doing something *with* someone, instead of *for* someone. Creating sex together, instead of being a vehicle for someone else's sex. It was not giving in but it was a giving with. Being penetrated didn't feel like an insult. I stopped pretending, felt what was happening and started to connect a little more to myself through him.

Once, early on in the relationship, we were having sex and I remember, with sparkling clarity, realising that I was having a moment of perfection, a moment of such profundity that it went beyond words. I remember feeling the safest I have ever felt with another person, and thinking, *This is how it should be. This is what goodness is. Remember this feeling.* I can't summon it now, but I can remember my big window and the sunlight dappling through the trees in the courtyard. It was daytime, and I can remember my small white IKEA table, his shoulder and his beard.

I liked being able to focus on S in a caring, loving way. I liked these parts of myself. It felt a little as if wanting him sexually wasn't really allowed, like if I expressed want for him, it would reveal some dark truth. But that became safe as well, and allowing my body to feel pleasure safely was profoundly healing. We were never *in love*. Our relationship was missing some connector, some quality of depth, but for what it was, it was very beautiful. One time, he came over to my apartment with a small bunch of roses, another with a tiny bear he'd picked up in a second-hand shop. I named it Schnecke Bär, which means 'Snail Bear'. I was always amazed that he would think of me when I wasn't around.

The world opened up to me in a way it hadn't before. It became softer. I couldn't self-harm with sex, which would have been so easy in Dublin. I had little to no belief in myself as an artist, but I liked my life. I felt delicate, and entitled to a life of my own. How do I explain the feelings of delicacy that were tingling through my veins? It was as if I was carefully making my way across a frozen lake.

S had been living in Berlin for a few years, and he brought me to his favourite places to eat, to see his favourite views, to play table tennis on his favourite tables. Even going on the train with him felt like a special journey. We went to a nearby lake called Schlachtensee, rented a boat and paddled about for a few hours. We went for hot chocolate in the fourth-floor café of a grim department store. We went to the zoo, the aquarium, second-hand shops. We ate Currywurst on the side of the road, like tourists. I lent him my Dylan Thomas short-story collection and he was unimpressed. We worked on plays together, making fake glass out of sugar to smash during productions of *The Goat, or Who Is Sylvia?*. We tried to source a dead goat. We held hands all the time, and I felt safe, safe, safe.

S went travelling for a couple of months, and when he came back the relationship had a different quality. I wanted a certain kind of intense depth and he wasn't a very intense person.

We broke up eventually, on the Friedrichshain Bridge. Every time I cross it during my annual visits to Berlin, I think of S and that day. I was devastated, even though

I knew it would end at some point. I had to confront the things I'd done, like absorbing him into my life so I wouldn't have to look at my own too much, and using him to distract myself from my simmering anger, my patterns of co-dependency.

I'd learned so much about how equal relationships work, about my capacity to love. I'd learned about respect and being respected, and I'd learned how to respect his feelings for me without feeling the need to offer something in exchange as compensation. It can be so hard to be a human: we are full of flaws, judgements, assumptions and urges to control. And all the stuff we carry from childhood. It is then so beautiful to meet someone who accepts all of that in you, who thinks you're worth it despite the mess of you. I feel profound gratitude for that relationship and for what S brought into my life.

While I was living in Berlin, I found a video online of a former porn performer giving testimony in court about her experiences in the industry. She was articulate and passionate, and her anger burned out of her eyes at everyone in the room. As I watched, entranced, I felt a heave in my chest, a burning knot in my throat and angry, hot tears in my eyes. My body felt as if it was trying to eject something. I felt so angry that I had the urge to break something.

I was taken aback by my reaction. This wasn't about me, it wasn't my story, but the rage had been simmering quietly within me, triggered whenever a man cat-called me or came on to me – any moment I felt that I was being objectified, leading to sometimes disproportionate responses of anger. This woman going up against the pornography profiteers, gave language to my feelings and experiences. She was telling the truth of herself. I felt a pressure zooming up inside me, barging out to my edges. It was my past. It was my own truth. Everything made sense and everything burst into life.

None of what had happened to me was okay. Sitting on the floor of my bedroom, I was aghast, in shock. I felt cold and scared, as if an outer layer of skin had been scraped off. And I no longer had the gentleness and tenderness of my relationship to be my buoy. I was alone experiencing this inner explosion, this ripping-apart. I sat there. *What happened to me? What did I do? Look at how one thing bled into another. All these men hurt you, and you were hurting yourself, and you could have been any girl.*

One day a few weeks after we broke up, S and I were having coffee in the sunshine at an outdoor café. I told him a bit about it all. I hadn't planned on telling him. It just came out. He didn't understand, so I explained. He is a very calm person and stayed calm then too. There was no drama. He hugged me. It was a long conversation, and it was a beautiful day with the heat of the sun on my skin on a cobbled Berlin street. I felt relief and lightness as I shared the weight of this thing that I hadn't even realised was hanging like a boulder from my neck. It was no longer *just something I had done*. It was real and present. Now, I had opened this bit of me, the invisible became visible: the pain and the regret of it stung, and I gently collapsed into it because S had made it safe to collapse.

I decided to move back to Dublin. With the discomfort I was feeling about my past and the breakup, I felt an urgent need to do something productive, structured and familiar. Being in unknown space isn't comfortable, but it is necessary, so that we can listen to and access the wisdom it has to share. Often we favour distracting ourselves to avoid the feelings it brings up for us. My personal speciality in this area is collecting academic qualifications. As soon as I got home, I started an intense full-time master's in broadcast journalism. I felt the familiar niggle of unease about it, but ignored it. *This is fine*, I told myself. *This is the right thing for someone like you to do*. Although I had been in Berlin for a little over a year, I felt as if I had moved much farther away and for a much longer time. I was emotional packing my bags with all the things I had accumulated. I wasn't saying goodbye to a city, or to S, but to the chance I had given myself to be free, to be an artist. And returning to Dublin was going home to the rest of myself, where the chances felt slimmer and where other stuff lived.

When I got back, I realised how recent, how present, what I had left behind actually was. The past was just a part of Dublin. It was as much a part of home as the road signs are, as the cobblestones are, as the trees that line the streets are. It lives in all the roads of Dublin just as it lives in all the roads of my body. I was distraught for a few months, as I adjusted to life there again, I felt an immediate pull back into exploitation. It felt too close to resist. That pull to re-enact trauma is difficult to explain. It was like a riptide underneath me, a draw, a current pulling me back to familiarity, where I know my role, where getting to know who I am isn't a thing I have to do. I was free, but I wasn't free. Holding trauma and freedom in one hand is tricky, as one tries to overcome and negate the other. I nearly got involved in the sex trade again, but I resisted. I made myself matter, even though I didn't feel I mattered.

I was cycling my bike when I saw a sign for a certain hotel and my chest seized – I was in the wide reception area, then in the lift. I had to stop my bike, get off and reorient myself to where I actually was, what I was doing, where I was going. Later that day, I sat with a friend in a coffee shop, and I had to look at every person who entered. I glanced at the door so often it was as if I had a nervous tic. I had to pretend to my friend that everything was normal, asking questions just to fill the tense space inside me. I told myself, *This might get worse*. I felt on edge until I got home.

Another time I was driving my car – and I saw a print pattern on bed sheets and my hand in a fist gripping them, as an elderly man fingered me so roughly and so fast that I could not breathe. I hadn't forgotten that man, but I had blocked out this part of it. It was a new memory, like a brand-new experiencing of it. I felt as if I was gaping open, with a huge hole in my torso. I pulled in and sat in the car with my hands on the wheel and took in air until I could continue driving. *That actually happened*. I told myself, *You were there for that. It happened to you. It happened to this body.*

I thought I was losing my mind. I went in to college to my master's every day, absurdly holding both my assignments, notes and new friendships in the same body as my refreshed memories and realisations. I knew I needed help but I didn't know where to find a supportive person who wouldn't judge or make assumptions about me. I'd read punters' comments on an escort website, giving out about an organisation that supports women affected by prostitution. I emailed them and got a call back later that day. About a week later, I met a middle-aged, dog-loving case worker in a café off O'Connell Street, and I cried and held my cup of tea.

'I'm sorry,' I said.

'Most people cry,' she said.

Maybe my pain is real, I thought. Maybe I'm not making it up or being dramatic or being self-involved, if this is what happens to most women she meets. Every now and then, I would drive out to the agency's office. They let me bring my newly acquired dog, and she mooched around the room while I spoke with the case worker. It was good having someone who understood how I was feeling, who understood how the impact of trauma lands later and who didn't judge me. My anger against the entitlement of punters and sex-trade profiteers grew and grew and was a ball of fury inside me. I wanted to change the world.

My journalism master's opened me up to the media, how accessible it is, and the possibility of having my own voice. Naively, I thought that my story alone would be enough to rebut a media narrative I was seeing repeatedly, which endorsed the sex trade as a legitimate part of society. I became aware of a journalist who had written in favour of the sex trade and those who profit from it. With this new-found awareness and my general naive trust in people, I contacted the journalist, thinking, *When he knows my story, he'll know that he's come to the wrong conclusions. He'll be happy to get everything clarified.* I believed in good journalism and journalists. I believed in people wanting to know the truth of things. I took the risk and called the journalist. He told me he would love to know more about my story.

'I'm an old man,' he said. 'I don't know how it all works any more.' He told me he didn't know any of the agencies that worked with women in prostitution. He told me he was clueless.

'You'll have to fill me in,' he said. He asked me where I lived, and I told him. He said he could meet me locally for a coffee. He was eager, and I was eager too, excited at this opportunity to set something right. I thought one article was all it would take to set right the others that had come before. Feeling pretty excited, I told my case worker about it. Her face dropped when I said the journalist's name.

'He knows all about us,' she said. 'He knows all about how the sex trade works. We've reached out to him numerous times but he refuses to talk to us.'

The truth churned inside me and everything made sense. How he related his lies, his tone of voice, his apology for being ignorant, his eagerness to get me into a room with him so he could use my story and naivety for some article that would no doubt have hurt me. In this particular sphere of my life, there was nothing like realising the betrayal of being lured in bad faith.

I gave the agency an anonymous testimony for its annual report. After the testimony came out, excerpts were used in several newspapers. One of the articles argued in favour of the sex trade. I came across it while sitting in a dentist's waiting room. The journalist didn't mention anything of my testimony until the end, where she quoted its last line: 'As long as prostitution exists, men and women will never be equal.' She said my contention was 'not only ridiculous, it's perverse'. I didn't understand why she had ignored the rest of my testimony. I couldn't understand why she had mocked what I had written. I googled the publication's address – I was so angry, I wanted to track down the journalist.

Didn't she have any idea of the amount of courage it had taken to write that testimony and allow my words to be sent into the world? Didn't she want to know about perspectives beyond her own? Wasn't she curious as to what someone in the sex trade had to say? Did she not have respect for such an opinion? Was I just stupid in hoping for that? My naivety crumbled away and I was left with nothing. I learned that not only were strange men not to be trusted, but I also couldn't trust the people assigned to tell the truth. It seemed the world was made up of exploiters, profiteers and cynical, malicious apologists. Again I got the message that I didn't matter, but it didn't bother me as much. Buoyed by the sense of having a voice, I started an anonymous online blog.

It was 2012, and blogging was relatively new. It became my online diary, a place where I wasn't just venting to my case worker. I ran my thoughts and feelings directly into it, and published immediately. At least a hundred thousand people read it. Comments came streaming in. One man wrote to tell me to keep writing; another said he'd been sent one post and stayed up for four hours reading the whole thing. I tucked their comments into my heart. What I wrote was raw and unashamed and angry. Punters came along and tried to be mean. I didn't care: they fuelled my rage. Nothing could touch me. The site was discussed on websites and all over social media; my posts were translated into different languages. People said their entire view of the sex trade had changed. Men and women from all around the world sent me their love. Other sex-trade survivors wrote comments; we connnected privately and I could breathe again. I exhaled into mutual solidarity. Sex-trade profiteers and apologists left desperate comments saying I was too good a writer to have been involved in the sex trade, that I was a 'taught' writer, hired to create a narrative. I was lied about all over the internet, wherever my blog was being discussed. It was extraordinary to see how threatening I was to those who would have preferred me to stay quiet. It was extraordinary to witness my own power.

Journalists wrote lengthy articles about my blog in newspapers and magazines. I was in charge of my own story and it was okay to be angry. I was making change happen. I was on fire, but fires die, and after several months I was burned out.

In September 2012, Jill Meagher was raped and murdered in Melbourne. She was a friend of a friend, and I stayed up late every night after she was reported missing, panic in my chest, checking the news, seeing her husband's tired face as he spoke to reporters.

When her body was discovered, I texted condolences to my friend and cried on my couch for an hour. I took the dog to the green with her ball and cried and cried, confused about the depth of my grief for someone I had never met. My last blog post was about Jill. I couldn't write any more. I could no longer be a one-woman holder of male violence. The enemy was too big, and I was exhausted under its incoming weight. I deleted the blog. *What's the point?* I thought. *You alone can't change anything.* But I had forgotten about another army: all the survivors I had connected with, all the activists around the world I had met during that time.

This is the best bit. I am not alone. I am part of something much bigger than myself. Whenever times are bleak, which is often – another woman raped or murdered, another suspended sentence handed down, another woman's underwear shown in court as 'proof' of her consent, another vicious lie spread, another sex-trade survivor disbelieved, mocked or threatened – and I feel dark and fatigued again, I remember that I know these women. I send them a message, reconnect with them, remind myself that I am not alone in this, that I never was. I am part of an invincible army, one that will never back down, and never give in.

... all I want is out there, waiting for me the minute I say I know who I am.

Arthur Miller, *Death of a Salesman*

RAPE, OR THE BEGINNING

I have a picture in my mind, a still frame from that night, a keepsake, truly a precious one. It is of the tall trees above me reaching, like arms, to the sparkling black sky, the world and everything in it happening underneath. It is so necessary to remember this vitality. We can hold multitudes – devastation, love and all in between – in the same moment.

It started when I was sixteen, but more likely, it started way, way before then. The assault was not the dramatic and violent affair that, later in life, I wished it to have been. Yes, I wished it to have been dramatic and violent. Mine was not a clear-cut 'stranger rape'. It was grubby, stained with my own failings, my own fingerprints all over it, as well as his. I had been drinking a lot, considerably complicating the purity of my victimhood. The perpetrator was also a teenager, a seventeen- or eighteen-year-old, equally drunk. Later, how I wished for an overtly brutal attack from a 'proper' predator. Somehow I instinctively understood the stigma of it. I yearned for knives, black eyes, defensive wounds, a hospital stay. Visible proof, and me therefore a visible victim. I yearned for big black headlines in the red-tops. I yearned for easy. Or as easy as could be.

I cannot forget him, his hair, his eyes, his narrow frame. He can forget me. I am a drunken memory. He probably did the same opportunistic prowling the next weekend with a different girl. Maybe she consented, maybe she didn't. He might have a family now. Maybe he feels defensive about the #metoo movement, but hides it because he thinks he's 'woke' and calls himself a feminist. Maybe he doesn't know he raped me.

His rape would go unreported, ignored, minimised and probably forgotten. It would emerge and be briefly acknowledged by my loving family two years later when I attempted suicide, then never spoken of again. This isn't anyone's fault. Sexual trauma can feel like a landmine – territory that is safer for all parties to avoid.

2000

Nothing bad has happened yet. There is a girl in my class called Una. I've been in school with her since we were seven years old. Una is tall and beautiful and has long, blonde hair. She doesn't try to hide her ignorance, her bafflement, her desires, her insecurities. She is delighted and mildly surprised when she does well at something in school. She plays hockey and gets really into it. She doesn't mind being very tall, while I, also tall, try to diminish myself. All of Una is just there, open for anyone to see, touch, get involved with. She is all of herself, all of the time, and I am jealous.

Una flicks through teenage magazines and stares at the pictures of male pop stars. She sticks their photos under her desk with Blu-tack. She is shameless in her adoration of boys. During break-time, she loudly compares the physical attributes of male football players, and I squirm nearby in discomfort. She applies make-up, right there in the classroom in front of everyone, and no one cares. She amazes me.

Una cries in response to anything emotional. Everyone mocks her mercilessly for this, but in a good-natured way, and she laughs along. I dismiss her emotional congruence as something weird, something to drawl *okaaay* in response to. I am annoyed at her blubbering. Why can't she keep it together? Does she have to be such an attention-seeker? I have a rigid sort of steely strength, and I control my many and complex emotional reactions.

I want to feel free to be 'seen', like Una is, but there is too much to lose. I obsessively read my horoscope in magazines in an attempt to understand myself. It informs me that to be a Scorpio is to be a boiling cauldron of emotion with a steel lid on top. I don't know how much I believe in these things but it seems to make sense. I *am* a boiling cauldron of emotion with a steel lid on top. If anything bubbles out, I clamp down the lid, mortified and ashamed that anyone might have got a glimpse of me. Una is not ashamed. She leaves the lid off, and it bubbles over, and she is loved for it. Una is definitely not a Scorpio.

Why can't I be like Una?

I try to be normal and fit in, and fake my way through my many inadequacies. I am too shy, too melancholic, too people-pleasing. I forget sometimes, and I am accidentally too loud, then funny, performative, then embarrassed, afraid that they saw too much.

I have no idea who I am, which is how it generally is when you're sixteen.

My birthday is in the slate grey of November, and my friend Sarah has brought brownies into school to celebrate. I step out of the beige Portakabin we use as a break room and she comes around the corner, holding a huge tin with the lid off, a candle sticking out the top. I am nearly sick with shock. She sings 'Happy Birthday', and some others milling around join in. *No need, no need*, I plead, wanting to die on the spot. The singing ends and we all stand around eating brownies. I am delighted and excruciatingly embarrassed. Then, I am embarrassed by how happy it makes me. I cannot stop saying thank you to Sarah. I want her to know exactly how much I appreciate her act of love. I nearly grovel with my appreciation. 'Okay, we get it, we get it! You're grateful!'

Sarah exclaims, interrupting me, annoyed that I can't just be normal and say thanks one single time, give her a hug, eat a brownie and get over myself. The way she snaps at me ruins the moment. Now I've annoyed her, now I've really fucked it up, and I've got to make it up to her somehow.

In second year of secondary school, a tabloid photo-journalist went to a teenage disco. He took photographs of some thirteen- and fourteen-year-old girls wearing tiny skirts and 'hooker' boots, pink boob tubes, belly-button rings and tiger-stripe highlights. He photographed them in compromising positions, sitting on boys' laps or being pressed into dark corners. We thought the girls were famous. The pictures were all over the front page, next to a scandalised headline. Beside it there was a small picture of a model in lingerie, with a promise to see more of her inside.

The first time I realised that men held the power was in 1995. I was eleven years old in a newsagent's with my friend. We had one pound each to buy sweets, so this was a serious undertaking. An older man, maybe fifty, was in the queue behind me, grazed his hand off my back and left it there with a gentle pressure, as if it was an accident, but it was too certain of itself for that. I kept my eyes on the sweets behind the Perspex display, the flurries of colour clamouring for my attention, organising my thoughts around getting the most value for the single pound coin I had to spend. An ice-pop or a hundred penny sweets? It'd be cool to have something for later too, to stretch out this rare treat, to savour it all day. Packets of Chewits or Frosties? Or loads of lemon lollipops? I was terrible at maths and my friend had nearly finished at the till, so I had to decide quickly and this man's hand was pressing between my shoulder blades over my yellow T-shirt and I was trapped until the fat woman in the navy apron shouted, 'Next!' I just had to ask for what I wanted and then I'd be back in the summer sun, comparing sweets and talking about anything but the man in the queue, like it didn't even happen.

Then I was wearing a sundress at fourteen, visiting my older sister in Hamburg, and a man on the street gazed at me, slowly looking me up and down. He had a wrinkle around his eyes and a smiling mouth. *That must mean he thinks I'm pretty.* What a thrill.

I was on the train into Dublin, age fifteen, when I realised that I was a sexual object by default of being female. An old man sat next to me and felt up and down my side for the duration of the journey. I was ignorant of the ways in which men can harm women and girls. Everything is new when you're fifteen. You take your cues from adults. I didn't have a cue for this, so I waited for the groping to end. I froze and stayed frozen.

You have a general trust in the world, and in adults and

in yourself, that events like these slowly erode. Those events turned strange adult men into potential predators when they had never had that connotation before. They turned my own body into a thing that could potentially bring harm to me. They transformed my first moments of sexual awareness into a seedy, shame-filled thing, which I was not consensually part of. I was forced into someone else's sexual life and fantasy, yet I didn't even have one of my own.

She remembers:
Shining eyes, eager eyes.
Wet grass, hard mud, cold.
Seeing her breath in front of her face.
The bark on tree trunks.
The black night sky, tree branches in silhouette.
The silky touch of an Adidas hoodie.

I am waiting for the bus. I'm wearing a big, grey hoodie with a ripped pocket, so everything always falls out, and a necklace with a shiny metal dolphin. I meet my three friends and their boyfriends at the off-licence; one of us goes in with a fake ID and gets the drink. We climb over a high, crumbling wall and sit in the deserted part of the unending park – the sky is stretching so clear and so high above us, as we open our cans and naggins.

The boy, Peter, has big, black pools of eyes, a sharp jaw, a slight frame and skinny fingers. He'd come breezing over to our group with another boy, radiating an easy-going, quiet confidence, and I feel okay about him being there, sitting in the freezing air, pretending I'm not cold. I feel included and normal. I warm up with vodka and cranberry juice, and maybe the potential of something happening here is warming me too.

Peter wedges himself between Sinead and me. I know from the way he's looking at me that he likes me. His dark eyes never seem to move away from me, like they're seeing through me. Every time I glance at him, he's already looking back, and I feel self-conscious but in a thrilling way.

I get drunker, and he holds my hand on the grass, and I feel like I'm melting. Everything is new, and I want to know.

Then he is leading me away to the trees on the outskirts of the park, and I let him. The grass is long, and sometimes I have to lean on him to stop myself from stumbling. I feel proud because his hand is holding mine. *This is what it is!* I think drunkenly to myself. *He likes me.* I wade through grass towards happiness, validation, the feeling of *I'm okay* that I grasp for day in, day out, towards the feeling of pure relief that I am likeable, lovable. His hand clutching mine balms my insecurities and whispers, *See? You're fine as you are. You're okay.* I believe this and, combined with the dizzying, drunken vodka fog, I feel very okay. Everything about the situation feels right. I've finally got it and I feel entitled to it. *I deserve this. Thank you, God, for finally letting me have this.*

We stumble towards the break in the high wall that surrounds the park. In the years to come, my memory of this will be distorted. The wall will be a hundred metres tall, scraping at the lid of the sky, with the yawning hole in its centre cluttered, not with rocks and stones, but with jagged boulders, a caricature of what it actually was.

We plonk down under some trees next to the gap in the wall. Night is coming, the air is darker, more still. Dusk is settling all around. My friends and their boyfriends stay far behind, sitting in the long grass in a haze of smoke. I can still hear the glasses clinking. Two of the three couples will go on to get married to each other.

My only experience of kissing boys so far is at a low-ceilinged, sweaty teenage disco where my mouth was penetrated by a swirling mess of tongue and teeth, braces and saliva, while stabbing little fingers try to rummage under my string top to reach my white bra. Peter's kissing is abrasive, truly bad. His mouth is sharp – all of him is so sharp. He is like a long-nosed rat, foraging and nibbling. My throat is ragged from all the smoking, and my head is molasses. It feels like I am spinning uncontrollably backwards towards the ground, afraid to close my eyes in case I might never open them again.

The stars are blinking through the tall tree branches and I feel simultaneously tiny and also the most important thing that is happening in this moment.

Peter paws at me with his thin white hands. I let him. I don't really mind. I don't consider what I think of it. Being drunk makes the unallowable allowed. It blurs things like instincts and the ability to speak.

But it's okay because he's kissing me, and I like that bit, even if he is abrasive, and I don't want it to stop. I don't want the attention to stop, the feeling of being wanted. So I'm willing to go a little bit further for it. I've never done anything like this before. I don't know what it will be like. *There is a first time for everything. You might like it.*

I try to make my face look better, try to pull myself together. His scratchy fingers get beneath my underwear. *Okay*, I say to myself, *this is what is happening now.*

The feeling of his fingers clustering in my underwear is a sensation I will be able to recall long into my adulthood. I will be able to summon it in seconds. The violence of it and my immediate acceptance of that violence. How I let myself down. My immediate acquiescence to the invasion. His cold fingertips on my warm skin, which has never been touched by anybody but me. *How pathetic*, my future self will hiss at this teenage self. *How pathetic that you let this happen.* I pretend I know what is going on. I don't want to look stupid. Above all, he can't know that this is a new thing for me. Being drunk is incredibly liberating. It lets me ease the constant monitoring, the censoring of my behaviour. I can be spontaneous. I can let go of questioning every single thing. I experience myself sort of freely, and I like this version of myself that is relaxed and cool and does things.

I haven't yet learned how to listen to myself, assert myself, how to say *Yes, please*, or *No, thank you*. Peter, too, hasn't yet learned how to listen. He rummages, and I let him. It is happening without me. Maybe he would leave me here on the grass if I rejected him. Maybe I would hurt his feelings. I want him to like me. And it's not that bad. Everyone does this. It's normal. How many times since have I swallowed my feelings so as not to upset or anger a man? Many hundreds, I reckon.

I go along with it, faking being fine with it, faking being cool and chilled, faking being into it, and, as I do, I feel myself closing, shrinking. And I feel disappointed. I stay where I am, but I wish the hand-in-hand feeling would come back, hoping that, maybe if I allow him more access, it might. I am lying so close to him but I have never felt so disconnected from another human being, and I don't understand how things have changed so quickly from the nice warm feeling to whatever this is.

The grass is damp and the mud is hard and cold. We are

lying on it, two teenagers under the moon on a Friday night, like so many thousands of other teenagers across the country, in parks and fields, on walls, in gardens, on beaches.

Peter says, 'Do you like it?'

I say, thinking I'm being cool, 'I'm not going to fuck you.'

I use the word 'fuck' as though I'm not a sixteen-year-old virgin but a person familiar with regular, casual sex, like a character in a television show, pithy and knowing. I use it like I'm used to using it, like a weapon, spitting it out.

I say to myself, *That's enough. You've drawn the line. Now he knows.*

But he doesn't know or doesn't want to know, and I'm limbless now. I have eaten my own tongue. I can do nothing. I tried. I tried and failed.

Body, I'm sorry. Insides, I'm sorry. Parts of me that were still a mystery to me, I'm sorry. I robbed you of gentleness and care, and I apologise. I let you down, body. The line I drew wasn't enough because the line was just words.

His face scrunches up, and he admonishes me, 'I wouldn't fuck a girl without a condom.'

His tiny, sharp, earnest face. *Wouldn't fuck a girl. A girl.*

Not 'you'. A 'girl'. Any girl.

I feel cold.

I can see his veins under the skin of his neck. Teenage blood racing around, flooding with excitement, a rush of blood. My blood is rushing too, pulsing in the back of my

174

head, banging between skull and cold earth, and I pass out.

I wake and feel pressure on my legs. Pressure somewhere else. I hear a shuffling noise, the friction of a jacket rubbing against me. I can smell something alien. Peter is raping me. So he *is* fucking me without a condom, after all.

I close my eyes.

My head has melted into the ground. The blood is stagnating in my legs and hips. I am feeling the kind of drunk that cuts off everything else. The kind of drunk where you may know what is going on, but from so deep inside your mind that you can't connect it with your body. You can rationally think about what is going on, you can quite soberly talk to yourself inside your mind, but articulating your thoughts or moving is like getting out from beneath a duvet made of tar.

I feel the sting of it. The sting and shove of it. A wrenching feeling, like I'm being pulled out from the inside. And another shove, and residual sting, like a scrape more than a sting, a sharp scrape, as if he wanted to scoop something precious from out of there and wanted every bit of it, like the way I used to spoon out those strawberry yogurts as a kid, and I'd keep scraping with my spoon until the pot was see-through plastic again. That is what it's like now. I am see-through. I am hard, unyielding, made of glass, my body shattering from the inside. I have never felt anything like this in my life. The pain takes my breath away. *Is this what sex is?* It's a pain that makes me want to curl into a ball, closed with no gaps, but I'm open and paralysed.

It feels as if the whole of me from where he has violated to my throat is ripped open to expose all my stagnating alcohol-infused dead blood, organs and guts. A glass girl with solid blood insides. I feel like I've been split in two. I *have* been split in two. Before and after this are now two different places. This night is one of life's punctuation marks. I was an un-raped sixteen-year-old, and now I am a raped sixteen-year-old.

I say to myself, *It will end soon.*

I say to myself, *This cannot go on for ever.*

I wait.

My blood seems to start moving again because, after Peter gets off me, I am able to pull up my knickers and all my limbs move back to my friends and over the wall and out of the park and up the road and onto the bus.

My mouth is slack. I turn up my slack mouth for my friends on the bus to disguise my loss, my grief, the bits of me that have been torn away, which they know nothing of. I sit on glass, perch above the shattered bits of myself. Pain sits in a lump in my abdomen, stubborn and rotten.

A friend on the bus says, 'Are you okay?'

I say, 'Yeah, I'm okay, but I don't really like that Peter guy.'

'Why'd you go into the trees with him, then?'

I have nothing to say. I don't know why I went into the trees with him. I can't remember any of the good feelings any more.

I don't understand.

I'm scared.

2009

I was twenty-five, living in Berlin and trying to work out why I felt that I had to keep secret the fact I had been raped. I was now a fully 'out' feminist. I was discussing rape and sexual assault, male apathy to sexual violence, and pornography, something I used to defend. I was raising the issue of male violence against women identified as a male problem rather than a 'women's issue'. I was angry with men for not doing anything about the epidemic of male violence. I didn't understand why they didn't care enough to take action. I felt very alone in my feelings and concerns. There was a lot of resistance to feminism. The climate was harsh. It was the birthplace of the expression 'Not all men are like that.' I started a Facebook discussion about Ryanair's ill-conceived

Christmas calendars, which featured female flight attendants in bikinis. The discussion was combative. Everyone was hyper-sensitive, especially those who accused me of being hyper-sensitive. Men I considered to be friends laughed at me for caring. I trawled through the comments and sighed. We had so far to go.

My anger was restrained because I needed to be seen as 'reasonable', not too blunt, not too angry. Angry women are seen as hostile and are dismissed. I didn't want to be dismissed: I wanted to be listened to. I didn't want to turn anyone off. Despite how rude some of them were to me about women being treated as sexual objects, sexual violence and so on.

I wanted my male friends to be on-side because I already knew somewhere that men hold the solution to the ending of male violence. I held back because I was afraid of coming across as too emotionally connected to the issue, as if being emotionally motivated was some terrible, embarrassing thing, which somehow detracted from the argument. I didn't want anyone to guess that I'd been raped. My fear of exposure was almost palpable. I could feel it rushing up my throat. *Stay quiet*, it said. *Stay still*. The fear told me to get over it, to relax, to stop being so uptight, so angry and emotional. I had so many feelings, and I didn't know what to do with them.

2001

Most of the time I have it blocked out but sometimes I spend a lot of time thinking about Peter and what he did to me. I think, I think, I think. I tell myself, *It was just sex*. I feel guilty and don't know why. I feel weak. I think I should be stronger. I try to make myself believe that it was fine.

I try to be normal. I sit on my bed and text a boy I have just met. I think about Peter. I open a clean page on my notebook. I have to rewrite what happened. I have to rewrite Peter.

I write his eyes. I write him holding my hand. I write him talking to me, smiling at me. I think, *Everyone does this*. I think, *This was normal*. I think, *You just got drunk and had sex*. I think, *He didn't mean to hurt you*. I imagine him as I go through my homework. I go through it all again, each look, touch and utterance, dismantling what happened into a narrative that I can be okay with. I remember him smiling. I smile back. *See? That's all it was*. This is my heart reaching out to his. He was a teenager like me. He'd been really nice. He liked me. It was so obvious. It was obvious to everyone. I was so drunk. He was just another teenager, like me, confused and insecure and probably trying to work his way through his thoughts and feelings, like I was. He didn't *understand*. He was only *seventeen*. How was he to know? He probably thought I wanted to. We were *already doing stuff.* I was so drunk, how was he to know that I didn't want to? Maybe I said it was okay.

I put down my pen. He'd held my hand. I look out the window at the sea. Maybe I said it was okay, but I just can't remember because I was so drunk. But I was unconscious. I am not stupid. I feel a sickness in my stomach and pick up my pen. But maybe I'm not remembering it right.

In sixth class, a lady came into school and told us about periods and about sex. It was a biology lesson. Nothing was said about feelings or consent or relationships or what the first time might be like or do to you. A few years later, I knew what rape was, sort of, because of films and news reports and television. But that was it. That was the sum total of my knowledge.

I went to school every day, and everything was normal. I did not tell my family about what had happened to me.

I was the youngest of five children, all of whom had already left home when this happened. I was six years old when my oldest sister left home for the UK, seven when my second eldest sister left for Germany. Now, I had no allies around me.

I remember feeling very alone during this time. I could not tell my parents. I could not bring this dirt into their world. They had done so much for me. They had given me such a privileged life. I couldn't be the bearer of this. The words were not going to form in my mouth because they hadn't been formed in my mind. I was being as normal as possible, careful not to raise suspicion that anything was wrong.

At home, I was like a chameleon, complementing the emotional states of those around me. I erased parts of myself to accommodate the feelings, thoughts and opinions of others. I was losing myself, allowing others to fill my blank spaces with themselves. Life felt out of my control but I became highly controlled. I had two emotional states, one public and one private, the public one carefully curated.

I was also afraid of getting into trouble. If I told them what had happened, then the fact that I'd been drinking heavily would come out. I was so afraid of being criticised. I didn't want to be given out to or blamed or told I should have done this or shouldn't have done that. Trauma can distort what is real, everything looming larger than it might actually be. There were times when I considered telling my parents, and the words rose like dust to my lips, waiting for permission to be expelled. After dinner, they would watch the news, and sometimes I would watch with them. I wanted to say, *Hey, guys, something happened to me a year ago, something bad.* But I never did. It would shatter the easy atmosphere of home and news-watching. I would have to present it in a way that preserved the predictable normality.

I imagined myself unable to contain it, my power handed over and away to others. I was the thing that had to be contained. It wouldn't do any good. It would only bring drama and things going out of my control. Control was very important to me. I needed home to stay the same. Telling them would turn home into something else. And it would turn me into something else. So I stayed curled up in the corner of the couch with the dog on my lap, watching the boring news.

Around this time, I started to get dull, thudding head-aches. I had them while I was walking the long corridor to the science lab, sitting in German class, baking cheese bread in home economics. I had them when I was legging it up to the art room in the rain, queuing for the grim roll and soup the canteen offered as lunch, going to the shop and back, listening to CDs in my room.

My mother was concerned and sent me to hospital to get tests done. The nurse put sticky things all over my head, and I had to breathe deeply. I went into a CT scan, and alone in the tube, I felt surreal, as if I was in space. I moved my hand around in front of my face to reassure myself that I was still alive. A voice next to my head told me to stop moving, and I felt embarrassed because I didn't realise I was being watched. They didn't find anything wrong with me.

At the back of biology class, an image of overhead trees

swam in front of my eyes. I felt a rushing sensation, thought I was going to faint, couldn't breathe properly. I panicked. I didn't know what was happening to me. Someone brought a brown-paper bag for me to breathe into.

One day Mrs Foley, one of my teachers, asked me to come and talk to her at lunch, ostensibly about what I wanted to do after school. Intrigued by this special attention, I met her in the library. I wasn't sure what I actually wanted to do after I finished school, but I knew not to get too ahead of myself, squirrelling away my secret desires to be an artist, an actor or a writer. I told her I'd like to be an English teacher and a poet on the side. I wanted to impress her with my reasonable, safe plan. I thought that was what she would want to hear.

'Okay, Mia,' she said. 'How is everything else? How's home?'

'Fine,' I said, immediately bristling at this unwelcome personal question.

'Okay, well ...' Mrs Foley was nearly wincing.

I stared down at my notebook.

'Some of the staff have been talking a little bit about you. We've been ... noticing ... that you're, eh, a little different or, you know, maybe that something is going on.'

My entire body flushed hot and I started to well up. I was going to cry and now I had infected my school life. I had infected how the teachers thought of me. I had infected my future classes with Mrs Foley. They had been talking about me, noticing things about me. School was no longer a safe place.

'Something happened,' I said, and tears spilled uncontrollably out of my eyes, and I was embarrassed and wanted to die, but I felt the beautiful relief of letting go. I was saying it now. My body softened in the library chair. It would be over now, this holding on tight, this bracing.

'Something happened,' Mrs Foley repeated. She was sitting ramrod straight now, discomfort written all over her body. Her eyes were huge behind her enormous round glasses.

I nodded, silently begging her to ask me what happened, to ask it in a gentle, lowered voice and to tell me it's okay and that I could talk to her. *Please just ask me what happened.*

'Right. Well. Will you talk to your mother about whatever it is that happened?'

She gathered her things.

'Yeah,' I said.

Satisfied, Mrs Foley got up and left, leaving me sitting there with my notebook embarrassingly lying open, my fountain pen sitting neatly beside it.

I tightened back up, swallowed. I was getting accustomed to swallowing myself.

Months passed and I hinted with certain people that something had happened. I felt pathetic and stupid. I didn't know what I was supposed to say. I didn't have the words. I never went back to that park and I drifted away from that group of friends. Everything was flavoured with something else now. Everything was contaminated. Good moments came and went – like essays, plays and debating; they did matter, they didn't matter. The things I loved seemed to be hurting because they were residing in my heart with the worst thing. And alongside the beautiful parts and the torturous parts there was banal, uneventful teenage life. Exams and cans on the beach, awards, small enthusiasms, minor heartbreaks.

I cared about friends and fitting in. I tried to be normal. Friendships came together and fell apart. My weird sense of humour started to slide. I was too self-conscious now to express any part of me. I wrote long and terrible poems about beams of sunlight splitting open rocks. I sat at the white desk in my bedroom and allowed the drama of the situation to exist in the safety of the page. I was getting smaller.

I am guilty. I am guilty. I am guilty.

I am toxic because my body has this rape lying under its skin, in my blood, inside me. I want to scrape it out. I carry the shame of Peter's crime within my very being. Shame soaks into my bones. Shame is now who I am. I wanted his attention and affection and passively accepted his aggression. The guilt settles into my bones and spreads from there throughout my body. I have done something wrong, therefore I am less. Feelings swell in my stomach and erupt as breathing difficulty or headaches or anger, so condensed and still that it renders me nearly catatonic. I started my period when I was fifteen. I'd been a woman for only a year when I was raped.

At seventeen, I was already unshockable. A friend confessed her bulimia to me after school one day. 'I knew you wouldn't freak out about it,' she said. I was valued for being a listener. I had a gift for listening and not judging. This was a good thing about me, I realised. It was a revelation to learn that this part of me was valued. My sensitivity could be a good thing.

Trauma, like rape, doesn't necessarily take over your life. But it drips into every aspect of it without you actually realising. And we deal with it in private and alone, and no one else can know because they might and frequently do ruin everything we are doing to stay 'okay'. Our problems are never just one thing, anyway. How you experience life is different now. Your trust in the world has been torn out of you. Life marches along, with this thing dragging in the shadows, just out of sight, like the uneasy feeling you are being followed, except no one is there.

One morning before school, I was walking my small dog, Molly. A neighbour was loading his enormous guard dog into the back of his specially adapted jeep. Molly was off her lead, trotting ahead of me, oblivious of the threat. We were both oblivious of the threat. Suddenly the guard dog was on her, flipping her over. Molly was swallowed under him – she didn't even get a chance to yelp. I stopped dead in my tracks, stunned. My small dog was being attacked, and I couldn't move. My neighbour roared over, beating his dog with a stick until it relinquished the terrified puddle of black and white. He got his dog into the back of the car but didn't say sorry. He didn't acknowledge my presence at all, let alone the violence of what had just happened. It was as if it hadn't even happened. It was as if Molly and I weren't even there.

I picked up Molly and carried her home. She had puncture marks on her pink stomach but her skin wasn't broken, and she seemed okay. I don't remember what happened then, but I do remember my shutdown, my inability to move, and how familiar this felt. If my neighbour was acting like nothing had happened, then maybe nothing had happened.

I watch my two-year-old god-daughter having a full-blown tantrum, standing in the kitchen doorway with enormous tears running down her face, wailing my name. Little arms at her sides, helpless (the shortbread biscuit is out of reach), but wailing. I watch her and think, *Keep screaming with your tiny voice. Keep owning your little bit of the earth, feet solid on the ground in your light-up runners. Keep wailing.*

The world was no longer mine to inhabit. Trauma disengages you from it, like after someone dies, and you find yourself lost in the supermarket, forgetting what you came in for. Trauma has to unfurl in easier-to-digest, bite-sized chunks. It has to eke itself out. You can't just heave yourself over it in one go. It won't let you, even if you try. So I did nothing, and tried to continue as normal and pretend that this intense sense of isolation wasn't really happening. I felt like a helpful visitor to life, but never a rightful resident with a life of my own. I was there to watch others, but not to be watched.

During this period I regarded my body with an aloof sort of detachment. I drew broken glass across its skin. I liked the feeling. I liked feeling as if I was in charge of how much it hurt. I could choose when and how much to hurt myself. I could stop the pain when I wanted. I was in charge, and it was only my body that I was hurting.

A rumour was going around that two of my friends, Ellen and Phil, had had sex. Sarah said it to me on the walk to the geography room.

'Did you hear about Ellen?' she asked, with importance in her voice and in her furrowed brow.

'No. What?' I said, always eager.

'Her and Phil slept together on Friday night. In Phil's house.'

She lowered her voice.

'His parents were away.'

My stomach dropped.

'Is that all?'

I dipped into the classroom before the conversation could continue. I felt heat on my chest and face, heat clawing at my throat. I was burning with hurt and jealousy. Ellen and Phil had been together since they'd met at a birthday party a year earlier. And now they had had sex. In a bed. Like normal people. At lunch, Ellen said how it was 'ideal' for both of them because they were virgins at the time. I smiled and nodded, then escaped the conversation and went out to the lane at the back of the school, so I didn't have to listen to it. My friends' collective naivety about sex hit me in the gut. It's just sex: it's just getting pummelled and shoved around and used. It's just nothing. That's what sex is: a scary, painful, meaningless thing.

I walked through the shortcut to the train station and saw a group of three older teenage boys coming towards me. As they passed, one grabbed my bum. It was so fast, I could have imagined it. I pretended to be annoyed, but really I liked it. My stomach tightened. I liked it; I didn't like it. I got onto the train and felt exposed and confused, because I was also experiencing a sense of power in being objectified. Maybe the ads and women's magazines, the music videos and the lads' mags were wrong. Maybe boys *could* like me. When van drivers beeped, I pretended to be annoyed but I was not. I felt a small thrill.

It was summertime and I was seventeen, and I was driving home in my sister's ancient Audi 80. I pulled up behind a long line of cars at a junction, the window the whole way down. A man selling magazines was making his way along the line of cars, offering a copy to every car. He wasn't having any luck. I could see a twenty-pence coin on the dashboard, big and bronze. I could see the horse on it. It wasn't enough to buy the magazine. I waited, reluctant to disappoint him.

He got to my window, and I smiled up at him.

'You buy?' he said, in broken English.

'No thanks,' I said, still smiling. 'I've only got twenty p on me.'

He stayed where he was, looking at me.

'You buy?' he said again.

'I don't have any money. Sorry.'

'Please.'

'I have no money, seriously.'

I tried laughing to relax the rising tension I was feeling. The traffic lights refused to change.

Then the man threw all the magazines onto my lap and pushed his upper torso through the window. 'For you, it's free,' he said. He reached beneath the magazines and between my legs and violently penetrated me with his fingers through my leggings.

I felt the solidity of his body against mine. I smelled his smell. I saw the individual hairs on his arm. I felt the magazines on my lap.

Somehow I moved one arm and pushed open the door. The man stumbled back and I threw all his magazines out after him. I rolled up the window and pressed my body back into the seat.

I looked in my rear-view mirror. He was gone. No one in

any other car came to see if I was okay. No one flashed their lights or beeped. No one was concerned that a man had just launched himself through a car window and emerged seconds later, followed by a pile of fluttering magazines.

I drove home. I berated myself for not closing my window when he became annoying. Shame and anger at myself spewed inside me. I had to make what had happened be okay and that meant blaming myself. I didn't tell anyone.

I had no language for sex, so I had no language for sexual assault. It was too embarrassing. I didn't want to bring my parents' attention to the private parts of my body. And if I did say something, I would be an open wound. They could do or say anything to me, and it might hurt me more. I imagined what they would say. *Why didn't you lean on the horn? Why didn't you just close the window? Why didn't you shout for help?* What if they told me how I should feel, and what I should have done, and what if they kept talking? This is why people use vague language when they're leaning towards telling a person that someone did something, that something happened. Testing. Asking: *Is this safe here? Am I safe? Will you please not be louder than me? Will you resist filling the hole in me with yourself? Just hold me up while this happens to me.*

I didn't see it as a crime anyway. Violence from men is the water in which women and girls unconsciously swim. I figured it was probably somehow my fault because I was now the type of girl to whom this kind of thing happened.

One night, late, when everyone is asleep, I creep downstairs and go into my dad's office. I turn on the computer and put in my earphones and wait for the dial-up internet to connect. I type 'rape porn' into the search engine. I am alert and jumpy, listening out for any sounds from upstairs. I'm not sure what I'm doing. Maybe I'm seeking some kind of answer to an unarticulated question. I scan through videos. I compare myself to the 'victims' in these videos. I scan and scan. What does rape look like? Did I look like her? Did I make those expressions too? How much did I fight back? Did I fight back at all? Is it still rape if you don't fight back? Is it still rape if you can't remember? Is it still rape if you passed out? What kind of rape victim was I?

I keep watching videos and the minutes tick by. I like seeing the women in sexual pain. I like seeing their pained faces. I am drawn to them. I like seeing them having no choice, no control over what happens to their bodies. I am on the side of the rapist. I want her to hurt. I want them to be hurt more than I was, to be in greater pain than I was. I want to see their feelings and feel their feelings. I don't want to be the only one. I want the pain to be okay. I keep searching, and the videos get worse and worse. I feel cold in my bones and realise I haven't moved my body in a long time, but I am transfixed by what is happening on the screen lighting up the dark room.

Then I find one of a naked girl, with messy blonde hair and pale skin, and I think maybe she is more like me than the others. I feel on the edge of something I am too young to understand, too soft to understand, aware somehow of the precipice I am on.

The girl looks back towards the hand-held camera with watery, vacant eyes because the man holding the camera tells her to. She is drunk or drugged or both. The man calls her a bitch as he fingers her. He hates her.

It feels like I'm watching a death happening. My hands are shaking from cold or fear or something else, but I'm invested now and I haven't got my answer yet.

I look at the expressions the girl is making and wonder if I had made those expressions too one year earlier. I don't know. I didn't see what faces I made. But I don't think my face moved much. I don't think I opened my eyes.

The man who hates the woman says something that is indecipherable to another man, and his voice is loud, presumably because of the proximity of his mouth to the microphone on the camera, and he's in my ear, so I lower the volume, glancing over my shoulder at the door, but nobody is up in the house at 2 a.m.

A disembodied male voice says, 'Bitch, turn around.' There is no other communication, and the silence is oppressive. Another man's torso fills the screen for a moment. He takes the girl's hair in one hand and puts his penis inside her. He smacks her. The girl's neck is strained but she isn't saying anything. Her eyes are half-closed. Her silence frightens me.

I didn't say anything either, and now I have a connection with this beautiful, blonde-haired girl.

Peter didn't smack me or call me a bitch or pull my hair. He held my hand as we crossed the long grass. It was an inescapable thing, a silent thing, save for the rustling of his jacket, and the sound of air leaving his mouth. He'd stayed silent too. I wish he had made a more human noise. If he had, maybe I could see him as a human.

According to Freud's sex-drive theory, humans have sex because they have an unconscious instinct to create life and avoid death. But pornography and rape are the destruction of humanity, making it more closely aligned with the 'drive' towards death, an unconscious desire to self-sabotage. In this context, sex is not sex. It is an edging towards death, fucking into death, celebrating death. This is the way towards death.

My entire body is shaking. I feel hollowed out, the inside of me like roots gnarling at a void that is sick for want of filling.

What happened to the girl isn't what happened to me. That isn't what Peter did. He talked to me about school. He'd given me some of his can of cider. He'd held me up as I stumbled over the grass. He'd held my hand.

But I have found my comrade in this thin, pale-skinned girl. Across the ocean, wherever she is, I am with her and, somehow, she has told me something. I have the answer I was looking for.

How can I begin anything new with all of yesterday in me?

Leonard Cohen, *Beautiful Losers*

TRAUMA

Sometimes I put J's name into Google. I do this maybe three or four times a year. Every time, I hope to see his boring, forgettable name on RIP.ie, but it never is. It's like he doesn't exist online. But everyone exists online somewhere. And sometimes I wonder if it all happened. Or if I made it up.

I type his name into Facebook and investigate each profile that pops up, hungry for clues. I know I'll never find him. I scroll down the long, long page of greyed-out faces on the profiles of those who choose not to have a picture, and it feels creepy, as if any one of them could be him, hiding there. And then I feel like a creep. I feel empty, as if I have a yawning pit inside me. It has been at least sixteen years since I last saw that man, but I still want to know if he's alive or dead. He floats into my mind most days, especially now, while I'm writing this book. If I gauged his age right, he'd be in his late fifties now. Potentially, I have lots of time to wait until he is dead.

I feel myself fall into a deep, dark well when I do this googling and death-wishing. I purposefully fling myself into it. I know I'm re-traumatising myself, but I can't stop. I watch every documentary and film I can find about rape and sexual violence. I like learning, so I tell myself it's learning. I devour all the psychotherapy resources on sexual trauma I can find. I do trauma trainings for psychotherapy. I buy books, listen to podcasts and interviews with trauma experts. I absorb as much as I can.

Sexual violence washes through my everyday life. I cling to rape trials, vicariously experiencing them and their injustices. A conviction gives me some temporary sense of justice-by-proxy, which I know I will never get for myself. I feel relief for the victim and relief for the country's women and girls. But someone has still been raped, and there will be another case the next day. Men's violence against women is overwhelming.

Being an abuse victim and also trying to be an activist is like being half-dead, half-alive. What keeps you going is the pain you witness, and what tries to kill you is the pain you witness. The vicious backlash when you speak about your experiences, the vitriolic lies about prostitution and its victims, the constant blaming, shaming and judging, the systemic normalisation of male violence against women, and the promotion of sexual exploitation, these things hold you underwater tethered to an anchor while your body desperately tries to float upwards. The part of you that wants to live free of it all will never get the chance.

Trauma is expressed relationally, in our reactions. We people-please, or are emotionally avoidant, angry and defensive. Clues for trauma are to be found in our everyday encounters. The older the trauma, the more ingrained the clues are within a given personality. Unresolved trauma shatters your sense of self, your relationship to your physicality, your identity. It infects your relationships. People, places and things start dividing up into safe and unsafe, and it is difficult to know which is which. People who were safe before may not be any longer. Places that were neutral are now loaded. Joy feels inaccessible. Spontaneity is gone because you have to make sure everything is safe. Saying how you feel in the moment is gone because you are shrinking away from life and you have to think about whether or not it's safe to say something first. It's only in recent years that I'm feeling the impact of what men did to me – the impact of what I thought at the time was consequence-free. And the more I realise that I matter, the more I experience feelings of worth, the more I see the past clearly, and this clarification is painful.

Dissociation is a way of coping with unbearable reality, a disconnection from the body and the present moment, spacing out, not being 'here', going somewhere else. We may grow so used to doing it that we become chronically dissociated. It is a safe retreat – as is feeling like an object – a diminishing of ourselves that is more secure to feel than the risky sense of our potential expanding openness into the world and its unknowns.

The realm of 'normality' is difficult. Talking about a friend's new job or what her colleagues are like feels banal and infuriating. It is as if you are a ghost being invited to discuss the weather, when ghosts are not concerned with the weather, and the more urgent topic, that you are now a ghost, goes unseen and unacknowledged. So you feel inept, unable to be 'normal' and connect, and you withdraw from others, and then you feel even more inept and unable to connect. Trauma means you feel alone, living your life alongside unwanted memories, physical sensations, feeling isolated, a fear of connection. You live alongside a precipice, between two worlds. I feel like a huge, black bin bag packed to capacity with trauma and shoved into a human shape.

My body remembers what has been done to it. The trauma is imprinted into my nervous system. It runs through all my senses. I don't like being touched by surprise, or when someone is too close to me or when someone pulls my top aside to look at a tattoo on my shoulder. I feel violated and am frozen from the inside out.

If a man is speaking to me in an authoritarian manner, my stomach flips. It infiltrates all my experiences. It's in being talked down to, raised voices and seeing 'dad bods'. It's in male road rage, street harassment and misogyny. It's in the bend of a neck and the cock of a head. It's in male entitlement. It's in laughter lines, crows' feet, gravity-drawn jowls. It's in having my experiences explained to me, rearranged for me. It's in questioning the behaviour and integrity of a victim and making excuses for the perpetrator. It's in the staggeringly unfunny memes my friends share online about teenage girls and Prince Andrew. It's in terms like 'alleged'. It's in wilful ignorance. It's in character references being read out at a rapist's sentencing. It's in the normalisation and acceptance of male violence against women. It's in the government giving €93 million to the horse- and greyhound-racing industries and €23 million across *all* domestic-abuse and sexual-violence services. Dogs and horses are more valuable to this country than the lives of women and girls, and the prior trauma is compounded.

Surviving does not end, but it feels circular. Some days I feel that I have been given a life sentence, and that life, and all that's in it, is slate grey. Trauma takes the colour from everything. Writing this book makes me feel as if all is barren. I have to dredge it out.

Trauma can be an everyday tedium, which is impossible to describe. I always thought that I lacked the ability to articulate it or to understand what I was experiencing. In *The*

Body Keeps the Score, Bessel A. van der Kolk states that he is in awe of those who can articulate the state of traumatisation, not telling the story of what happened, but the actual state of the impact. He says it is impossible to explain; it is beyond words. When I read this, I furiously underline it twice.

'Recovery' means to recover something that was lost, taken or given away and, in its absence, we grieve the losses. I wonder what has been lost that I need to reunite myself with. My experiences have cost me so much – the ability to trust myself and others, the ability to feel safe in relationships with others. Sometimes I wish I could float back in time and make different choices, although it was never going to be any other way. But I wish it could have been different. I wish I could whisper to my nineteen-year-old self, *This is going to hurt you for a long time and in ways you cannot imagine now.* I wish I could tell her, *You are attributing way too much power to this man. It's a trauma thing. You've been traumatised and you need to just stop for a minute.* I wish I could tell her how beautiful she is, how perfect, how funny, how talented, that she doesn't need constant validation. She doesn't need to feel a faux power over men. I wish I could tell her she already has power, the power of being her, the power of being alive and that she doesn't need anything else.

The state of trauma can also feel safe. I sometimes fear
I have identified so much in my sexual trauma that it has
taken over who I am. I'm not sure who is underneath it. My
experiences have impacted upon how I advocate for myself –
on even seeing advocating for myself as a possibility.

The tragedy of trauma is that it can derail us, sometimes
permanently, from our life's purpose, from who we were
supposed to be. Living out of the trauma has squashed my
heart's desires, my talents, my writing, my creativity, my artist
self. All have been muted as this multi-faceted trauma took
precedence. It has dictated the work I do and how I use my
spare time. When I could have been making art, I spent years
writing testimonies, submitting reports, giving talks – doing
anything I could to banish the darkness, so I wouldn't have
to live alongside it. Only now am I clearing space, welcoming
in the trauma. Come on, ruin the rest of it, ruin the rest of
me, obliterate my ego. And, in the ruination, maybe we can
begin again. And we can find a balance. It doesn't have to be
one thing, or another: we can integrate it all.

I think the world reveals something after a profound act.
A veil is lifted and you can see more of it. We rage and cry
because we have been badly hurt, and that is welcome, of
course. We don't want to see under the veil. It takes time to
get used to seeing everything anew. We try to hide from all
the raw truths – personal truths, family truths, relational
truths, societal truths. We must be patient and compassionate

towards ourselves as we ease our way unblinkered into our new world.

You learn how to negotiate the new world. You organise around the loss and there is a gradual losing of the things we have accumulated. There is a dynamic of trauma that involves the victim attributing too much power to the perpetrator as we remain trapped in our earlier, younger lens. A lot of recovering is losing the story of the perpetrator, seeing him not as an all-powerful, all-scary man, but through adult eyes.

Another dynamic involves the parts of you that believed the messages he gave you about yourself – his attitudes, his reasonable arguments. This is tricky. It takes time to disentangle his voice from your own and listen only to your own being. The centre of you sits beneath your thoughts, your physical sensations, your feelings. This wise centre is beneath everything that clutters the surface. If we can become familiar and comfortable with pausing and breathing, allowing the chatter to dissipate, we can clear space for our inner self, the self that is underneath the trauma, to be revealed. What we recover are the parts of ourselves we had to reject in order to survive.

Trauma resolution isn't an individual activity: we need our communities to support us. The impacts of healing take place on the individual and the community level. The invisible has to be surfaced for it to be resolved. By surfacing the invisible within myself, I surface the invisible that weaves its way through culture and society, through family, friendships and community dynamics, and through our thoughts and beliefs.

The journey of recovery, which could also accurately be called 'awareness', stops, starts and goes 'forwards' and 'backward', and which feels contradictory, will begin only when we are able for it to do so. We can't rush it or force it or make it happen to align with our lives. It will come up for attention when the conditions are right. The best thing we can do is turn towards it and acknowledge it. This is what is happening now and it's okay. Trauma is not a life sentence. We are not ruined. Sometimes the depths of our own beauty, others' beauty and the world's beauty are revealed only because we are compassionately present to our traumatised parts, because we are facing into our distress.

People who have not been traumatised, who experience the past as belonging in the past, can lovingly encourage us to 'move on'. Non-traumatic memories live where they belong, tucked into the folds of a history.

But trauma, like deep grief, remains alive in the cells of our bodies. With a memory, reminder or physical sensation, those parts of the past zoom up to our edges, and we are stunned again, experiencing the present through an aura of the past. It is like being haunted. Much of my work on myself has been on letting go of experiences, of stories, of memories, of attachments, of old narratives.

It is really hard to tell yourself to 'let go' and expect it to happen. The first stage is to hold the thing in your gentle hands with curiosity and love and acceptance that you are holding it. Then you might be able to let it go, but not before. Trauma can feel like we've been splintered. It can feel that way because, as the trauma memories or sensations or feelings jab at us, other parts of us get quieter, and we lose our sense of equilibrium. We just need to find it in the present, compassionately welcoming the traumatised parts and reintegrating the exiled ones.

The ironic thing about the feelings and thoughts we try to reject is that once they feel safe to exist inside us, just to be acknowledged with neutrality, they usually relax a little. We move on with, not from. You don't need to become 'whole' – you were whole before, during and after whatever happened to you. You just need to come home to yourself underneath the pain inherited from your experiences.

When we work with trauma and abuse, we are working in places of darkness and death. To relieve the suffering of those in the dark and dead places, we must face into and welcome what is dark and dead within ourselves. The friend who struggles to be with you in your despair, simply does not have the capacity to meet their own despair. It is only when we know our own darkness well that we can be present to the darkness in others. It is only when we have accepted our own shadow that we can be a safe refuge for others who are struggling with theirs. We cannot be compassionate towards others until we have sat compassionately with our own dark places.

If we want to transform the world, we have to transform ourselves first, and that means doing the opposite of what we usually do, and ushering in our darkness, letting the things we defend and protect be exposed and vulnerable. This can feel frightening and humbling. It allows us to detach from our protective egos and helps us to connect with others in a more open, accepting way, without being attached to how others behave. We notice more and judge less. We grow to learn that none of our internal experiences actually mean anything about who we are. If we live life defending and protecting ourselves, we'll never get to know ourselves and we'll lose the opportunity to reach the gold that is hidden in the things we keep in the shadows. The things we are most afraid of finding out about ourselves are the things to face into. When we learn to observe our ego and accept our stuff as it shows up as a passing natural occurrence, we stop being so precious about ourselves. We can take ourselves a lot less seriously.

It is easier to recover from the rape, because I didn't collude in being raped. I colluded in everything else. At least the rape was black and white, part of a world I could understand, where people make bad choices, and where there are perpetrators and victims. Getting raped was out of my control. But, later, with J and his friend, and then with all the punters, I chose to be there. I chose to reply, 'Yes, I'll be there.' I offered myself up for abuse. And even though I understand how and why we recreate trauma, and even though I understand now what I couldn't then about these 'free choices' I was making, I am still steeped in shame because the part of me that wanted to be treated badly was absorbed into my sexuality. But this is the impact of trauma.

Re-enacting trauma means putting yourself in similar situations or places to the original trauma, or finding similar people, and to create a new narrative in an attempt, this time, to be in control, to write a new ending, one in which you are in charge, not victimised. The sex trade is the perfect place for the sexually traumatised to try unconsciously to resolve former hurt because an unending number of men want to use your body. This is one of the reasons those who have suffered sexual abuse are so prevalent in the sex trade.

We don't know this is happening because it is an unconscious process. When you are experiencing the disconnection of trauma in your immediacy, you do not necessarily know it is traumatic because your mind and body are trying to survive. There is no safe space into which what is happening can be absorbed. There is no space for feeling or reflection. Our awareness is limited to what is tolerable. I have no need now to defend the 'industry' built by men for men. I didn't know why I felt as I did at the time. I didn't know why, sometimes, I would find myself crying for no reason. It is like trying to get through a swamp – all I could see was what surrounded me. You need distance to see the swamp as a whole.

When I was a child, I used to think about animals in the wild living their lives, how unfair it was that if they were impaired, they just had to limp around and hope for the best. I thought about sick crows and injured foxes. I thought how lucky we as humans are to have so many resources that we can mind ourselves in warm houses and hospitals when we are unwell.

In my work as a therapist, I have come to the realisation that we are no different from the crow or the fox. Life is as cruel to us as it is to them, albeit in different ways. I work mostly with women who have been raped or sexually abused by their friends, brothers, partners, fathers or strangers. The injustices are nearly too hard to bear witness to. I take conscious breaths with them in the presence of unbearable pain.

Too many clients to count have revealed child sexual abuse, sometimes after decades of holding the secret close, only to be blamed, shamed, ostracised, or for the abuse to be minimised or ignored. I feel most helpless and distressed when I'm working with young people whose parents are not able to love unconditionally. Witnessing the effect that has on them can be close to unbearable. This is how life can be, and we don't get to control it. There is not much we can do to ensure safety. A domestic-abuse survivor told me, "'Why not me?' is actually a better question to ask than 'Why me?'" The acknowledgement that what happened had nothing to do with the victim is where hope lies. We can stop struggling with figuring out what it 'means' that this happened to us and refocus on ourselves in the present: how we want our lives to look, what we deserve that we are lacking.

Child sexual-abuse survivors are the most courageous people I have had the privilege of sitting with. For some, coming up the stairs into a room where they will be met with someone who has a genuine delight in them and unwavering acceptance is a radically courageous act. What has been guaranteed safe in the past has not always been so. Safety itself feels unsafe.

Trauma makes us do weird things, things of which we are ashamed and which we keep hidden. Shame is just part of it. I tell myself it's okay to feel it. I breathe and let the shame exist within me. I tell myself, *I was vulnerable because I was raped.* I tell myself, *I was vulnerable because a predator primed me for selling sex.* I tell myself, *If he hadn't paid you, the rest wouldn't have happened. It wouldn't have entered your mind to sell sex.* I tell myself all this, but it rings hollow. I think I am the lowest of the low because of my past. I put myself in the same social category as a paedophile. But I didn't hurt anyone except myself. I didn't kill anyone or push drugs or abuse anyone. I never wielded power over another.

The shame seeps into my relationships. I sit with my therapist and feel myself freezing with shame. I barely move or speak, not wanting to draw any more attention to my physical form than is necessary. I feel shame about being a body in a room with him, as if it must be insulting to him, the pureness I have projected onto him. I feel embarrassed about telling him that I like yoga and swimming in the sea. I feel shame that my favourite alcoholic drink is Guinness, so I tell him I like some other drink instead. I feel so much shame in being seen by somebody else. I am waiting for my fear to be shown to me, that I am nothing, something to discard.

Sometimes, going to therapy feels like an endurance performance-art piece that I am endlessly rehearsing. Practising being seen, practising saying what I would like in my life, the really hard things to say, practising not being passive. Practising trusting myself.

When I bake biscuits for my dad and hand the tin to him, and he immediately takes one, sometimes my eyes fill with tears, and I have to look away from him. *If he only knew*, I think. *If he only knew the dirt of you, he wouldn't be here. He wouldn't care about the biscuits you made. He wouldn't love you. Nobody would love you.* I tell myself that he loves me. That he does love me.

I have unconsciously created stupid rules for myself. I have to be a strong person for those who feel less certain and less safe in the patriarchal world, for those less sure about the emotions that surface in them, for those easily crushed by the criticism and judgements of others. I have to be a rape survivor who gives light to other rape victims. I have to be strong. I have to be brave. I have to show that there is life after rape. My veins have to be hewn from steel. If I am anything other than the perfect rape survivor, I am not to be trusted. I would be seen as broken, and I wouldn't give hope to anyone. They would just see the brokenness. People would think I must be a terrible therapist.

The thing about shame is that it comes from someone else projecting their own shame on to you. When another person judges or shames us, we can choose either to buy into it or just notice the new information about that person's internal world of self-criticism and sense of shame.

The more we trigger someone's own shame, the more they will try to shame us.

We don't feel shame if a dog bites us or if our car has been stolen. It helps to know that the shame is not mine, but something I have unconsciously absorbed from someone else. *There it is again*, I think, when I feel it under my skin, *the men's shame.* And if we do the opposite of what shame is telling us to do, it learns that it has no place to live inside us. If shame is telling us that we don't matter, we have to do the things that matter to us anyway. If shame is telling us to stay quiet, we must speak up. If shame is telling us that we are insignificant, we have to do things that feel significant to us. If shame is telling us that we must obey perceived authority figures no matter what, we must rebel. If shame is telling us that this secret must never get out, by all means share the secret. And eventually shame will find no home inside us.

Shame is uncomfortable, but it is also an arrow pointing us towards what is underneath it, which is usually a judgement about ourselves. Shame tries to make life so uncomfortable that we take action. Shame is really trying to help us heal the hurts. In this way, if we can be compassionate towards ourselves in experiencing it, we can see shame as a friend, not a foe. It is rebellious to fling the things we are most ashamed of into the broad daylight. People don't care as much about the explanations for our choices as they do about witnessing another owning their stuff. It is what gives hope and spreads courage.

Five or so years ago, I organised a meeting with some good friends so I could tell them what had happened to me. It was becoming too painful to have a secret world and to limit and restrict how I expressed myself. I needed their support. Some of my friends had already known for a few years. I had told Ruth over chips and tea in a pub on Thomas Street, and Daisy in my art studio on Francis Street. I just said it, and there was no fanfare. Nothing fell apart.

Eventually, in the farthest corner of the unlikeliest pub, I told them about my past. I told them all in one go, so I wouldn't have to throw myself into feeling the same vulnerability and anxiety over and over, and it was fine. Everyone just listened to me, and I didn't feel any excruciating shame. For shame to thrive, it needs secrecy, judgement and silence. *Maybe I bring more than rape, sexual abuse and prostitution into the lives of those I love*, I thought. I remind myself that, to them, I am a normal person.

I'd spent so long trying to convince myself that my story didn't matter, that it wasn't 'bad' enough to tell, that I wasn't enough of a victim. My story was simultaneously not dramatic enough and too dramatic to tell. But in telling it, I have learned that what happened to me matters, and therefore that I matter, that I am not the sum of my experiences, and that 'You are the sum of your experiences' is a vastly inaccurate and deeply unjust statement. We judge people's characters based on their behaviour, but our character is underneath our trauma-responding behaviour. Our 'character' is usually visible in how we respond to *how we have responded* to trauma. We are not what happens to us. We are not even what we do with what happens to us. We are more than all that.

If trauma is the profound disconnection from yourself, then I'm reaching around in the dark, trying to find all the parts of myself. I am trying to find out who I am. I feel as if I could be anyone, that I could easily choose any role. I wonder who I would be if everything hadn't happened. When I was a teenager, I wished I could know how my friends would like me to be because then I could be like that and would no longer feel insecure. Back then, it seemed such a reasonable solution.

I still don't know who I am. I am unable to do small-talk, though I wish I could. I sort of fake it, which seems to work. I want to know people's emotional lives. I want to know what is underneath someone's hatred of a work colleague. On a writer's retreat, someone was talking in the group about a detailed and vivid dream she'd had the night before.

'What were you feeling in the dream?' I asked. 'When do you usually have that feeling? Where else do you notice it in your life?'

Eventually I realised that the woman was becoming self-conscious, and the small group was totally silent. *You've done it again*, I berated myself, *alienating people with your intensity and probing. Not everyone enjoys this kind of conversation.*

It's that I want to know the truth of someone. Trauma survivors greatly value the truth. We have been gaslit and lied to. Our realities have been mangled and twisted and steamrollered, ignored, manipulated and muted. I am a human being: please honour me with the truth. The psychotherapeutic relationship is truth-telling. You get the chance to be truthful in a way that can be trickier in other relationships. As the therapist, you can name your scepticism and be playful in response to a client's defences. You get the truth of the person when they feel safe. Then we can go anywhere on a foundation of trust. It is so important for women to tell the truth of their lives. It doesn't matter what your story is. Just tell the truth of who you are.

How I am in any given situation depends on the energies of the people around me. One-to-one engagements always suit me better because I can be present to that person and adjust easily to their presence.

Groups are different: I cannot adjust to so many people at the same time. I feel uncomfortable because I have no single person to focus on. My sense of 'how to be' is tied up with who is around me and their expectations, perceived or otherwise. It is a useful skill for a therapist but not as the overarching pattern for all relationships. I have to feel for the inside part of me, the who of me. To protect others from discomfort is written into my bones. I still haven't learned how to let others weather my storms with me. I still haven't learned that I can be the source of chaos. Sometimes, as I move from being a constant accommodator of anyone and anything to trying to uncover what is beneath, I feel like a non-person, just a blank, staring weirdo with no personality. I have to risk being seen, even if I don't know what is going to be seen. It is as if I am learning how to become.

Loneliness is like a heavy blanket draped around your world. It seems that everything is heavy, every leaf on the ground, the rubbish strewn about the bin outside the shop – everything is imbued with loneliness. When I'm feeling the dull ache of loneliness, it's almost as if I'm not really walking on the path in front of me but as if I'm in some sort of bubble, like the pope-mobile. I glide around disconnected, mechanical. I meet people and speak with them, but it's an act – my smile drawn on, my words laboured, my impatience muted out of politeness. I just want to be at home, alone, where I can hide.

There are times where I walk a thin and scratchy line between living and erasing myself as if I am a pencil mistake. Even when I feel most isolated, most withdrawn, nearly vanished, things happen that remind me that I'm alive, and it's always because of connection. A friend texting me something stupid and inconsequential makes my life suddenly matter, and I'm looking down at my phone, engaged in the present moment, and that is what is important: the immediacy of life and the immediacy of connection. Finding something funny, remembering that I have a sense of humour.

I resurrect all the other things in my life and try to make them stay in my mind: my friendships, my relationships, my school-time victories and disappointments, my humour, the way I loved performing and to entertain, my pets, the giant heart I made out of steel and chipper chips in third year in NCAD, which I lit from the inside with a huge bulb so it looked like a worshipping of love. I try to cement them, just as the traumatic things have been cemented. I have to remember the other things.

As I type these words, my friend Riadhna is upstairs in my bedroom trying on one of my dresses. She's shouting, but I can't hear what she's saying. All the parts of life matter. Living isn't an arbitrary accompaniment to my mind. I can exist in it. I can hold it all at the same time.

Sometimes I feel that I make my home and garden as beautiful as possible to shield myself from the constant rape and male violence in the world – the constant rape and male violence inside myself. Recently, I completed a questionnaire for a migraine study and one of the questions was, Do you experience joy?

I sat there thinking, *Oh, my God, never. I never feel joy. My internal life is a grey nothingness* – except, I realised, when I'm doing things in my garden. I take heart-swelling pride in seeing flowers bloom every spring and summer. I go to the garden centre and spend too much money, taking ages to choose new flowers for my window boxes and hanging baskets. It feels so wholesome that my heart wants to burst. I make up stuff to ask the staff about, just to talk to them. I go to the garden shop near where I live and ask for houseplant advice. 'Give it a haircut,' the guy says, about my failing String of Hearts plant, and I laugh, way over the top.

My friend Claire gives me cuttings of her houseplants all the time, and I tend them carefully, harassing her for advice. 'How much water? How much light? What type of soil? How do I know when to move them into a bigger pot?' Watching them grow is deeply satisfying.

In the summer, I bring my laptop out to the garden, sit there with a coffee and look at the flowers. The sun has lit one half of the garden and the other is in the house's shadow, and the flowers are like little floating buoys in the darkness. On one side, the petals and leaves are flinging back the light at me, so bright it is nearly blinding. And it's like I'm between worlds, and I feel as if I'm on the threshold of something but haven't grasped the meaning yet. It doesn't really matter: bright flowers can still be seen poking above the shadows, and there are others in the glare of the light.

I have reluctantly come to accept that I have to be the most important thing to me. I test trusting myself, see if I am still okay, test a little more. I do not need to know the world is safe before I put myself into it. Writing this book is the biggest act of trust I can make. My story is out of my hands now; how others respond to it is up to them. I will keep trusting where my heart is trying to take me, where I am being drawn to, and keep trusting that my story will be held because I know that I am the safe place in the middle of it all.

I like reading psychotherapy texts about trauma recovery to see if I can picture myself there, if I can trace some sort of a path. Judith Herman, the author of the seminal *Trauma and Recovery*, says that recovery unfolds in three stages: 'the establishment of safety', 'remembrance and mourning' and 'reconnection with ordinary life'.

I pine for ordinariness. I select parts of everyday life and become present to them. Driving my car to work, paying for petrol. I walk the dog every day, the same beach, the same rocks. I water my flowers. I make coffee. I text my friends. I talk to my neighbours over the fence. I vacuum the house. I bake. These are all ordinary things I do. I take life one breath at a time. I put my hand over my beating heart and listen to the kids outside the window, the cars starting. Children are the best for providing ordinary nonsense, so I visit my god-daughter and play with her. I am okay. The extraordinary ordinariness, the sacred ordinary.

Most mornings I start at five thirty or six and sit there thinking for a while and write. I use this time of the morning because I am much clearer and more still at this time, before daily life finds its way in. There are no car doors slamming or people shouting outside yet. My dog is still asleep. And it is still dark. I write until the neighbourhood kids are going to school and daily consciousness starts to invade my bubble. Then I do yoga, pranayama and meditation. It takes for ever, so some days I don't do it all. I have reminders of compassion around my house, like little statues of Buddha and the goddess of compassion, Guan Yin. A picture of the spiritual teacher Ram Dass in my living room reminds me that 'It's all perfect', whatever is occurring. These things are really reminding me of who I am when things get rough and I'm scared of the future, the times when I want to evaporate. The Buddha statues remind me that I am not this ego reaction: I am underneath it.

There is an uneasy pressure on people to learn and grow

from adversity, not to dwell in the discomfort it brings up in others – to keep that dark and miserable part private and to make public the inspirational warrior in you that survived and now has precious wisdom and, crucially, positivity to bestow: a reframe. I have no reframe of what happened to me. I have no wisdom to offer, except this: allow the darkness in and observe it, because quiet self-awareness helps us make mindful choices, rather than acting on auto-pilot or out of our survival system.

Although focusing on healing and integrating the impact of trauma helps many survivors and their supporters, it must also be acknowledged that not everyone can heal in their lifetime. For some, too much has happened, or it is too complex, or they do not have access to resources.

There is a cultural idea that if we have been traumatised, which all of us have to some degree, then we must 'take responsibility' and do the task of healing. This is fine, but it misses the point if we engage in it while holding ourselves or others under pressure to 'heal'.

First, we could just accept ourselves as we are, neutrally acknowledging what it is like to be who we are; noticing the various parts that show up in any given context. Trauma first needs to be accepted and met just where it is at, without pressure to heal or recover. The only task is to be. It can be perpetuated by pressure to change, just as it can be soothed by the respect and honour of pure acceptance. 'Of *course* you feel this way', you could say to your traumatised or otherwise hurting part. 'That makes perfect sense.'

Andrew Solomon spoke about 'forging meaning and building identity' in his 2014 TEDTalk. He said, 'Forging meaning is about changing yourself. Building identity is about changing the world. You need to take the traumas and make them part of who you've come to be, and you need to fold the worst events of your life into a narrative of triumph.' The 'triumph' is in dropping the struggle to avoid and embracing what is.

You have to fight for yourself every day and nurture what is good, whatever that is: compassion, love, a friend, a garden, a dog. You have to hold on and know that this impermanent inner turmoil and hardship will pass, and come back and pass again, as every sensation does, and know that there is more to you than this one experience. Surviving means allowing yourself to feel and experience it all, knowing that there will be a break in the weather at some point, and that when that break comes, a new and gentler weather system may appear.

I was given adversity, which taught me understanding. Confusion around my past choices shows me clarity in the present. A sense of isolation invites me to value connection. Loneliness invites me to attend to my heart. Witnessing the darkest darkness in others and myself has taught me compassion, that I am capable of making space for darkness that I can hold it for others. It grants me the need to wake up to myself so I can encounter life in a deeper way and have an altered experience of life thereafter. What is important now is not *Am I enough? Am I acceptable? How can I prove my worth?* It's *Am I loving? Am I loved? Am I telling the truth?*

The core of my life is the connections I have with those around me, to give love and to be loved. To love and to love and to love. I'd say that it's pretty universal, that the meaning of life is one another, the people in our lives who feel like home.

I'm going to make what happened to me matter. I'm going to make it matter beyond me and my life because what happened to me is so much bigger than me. I am determined that the knowledge I can impart is going to protect women and girls. Adversity is what creates the helpers and the healers, and I am a helper and a healer. I declare myself. I fling myself out into the world. My complex, messy self will be seen. I am not a rape survivor or a sexual-exploitation survivor or a former prostitute. I have found a part inside myself that refused to acquiesce. I am a person trying to conduct an act of service with this book. I am a person discovering myself. I am a person at a laptop writing some stories of my life. I am a person holding her dog in her lap. I am a person feeling nervous about the future. I am a person talking to her strawberry plant. I am a person drawing pictures in chalk with her god-daughter. This is who I am, as I exist from moment to moment, from my first breath to my last.

The cave you fear to enter holds the treasures that you seek.

Joseph Campbell, *The Hero with a Thousand Faces*

LOVE AND MEN

When I was living in Berlin, my then boyfriend would repeatedly tell me that when he got an erection it didn't mean I had to do something about it. He said it would go away on its own. I had no idea this was the case. I thought that if an erection happened, it wouldn't go away without ejaculation, and if the erection happened because of me, I had to look after it.

I dissociate during sex. Dissociation feels like an uncomfortable but safe refuge. I don't have to be present: I can zone out, go through the motions. I can watch and not experience. I can come in and out of whatever is going on. Dissociation means you can endure anything. I am not inside my body experiencing it, but I am outside watching the man, his facial expressions, his body movements, his veins, his skin, his muscles, watching how his mouth opens and closes. I watch impartially, as though he is a museum artefact I am inspecting with curiosity. My body does not feel much. I cannot relax into it; I cannot feel safe inside it. I am a stranger to it. I have learned how easy it is for me to experience anything simply by stepping outside my body and watching as whatever unfolds.

If I really know and trust the man, I can make myself return inside myself. It is an active choice I have to make, a radical choice to be present. *Stay here*, I tell myself. I feel his skin on mine. I feel the bedclothes. I touch his hair. I try to focus on the feeling of him inside me. I try to feel it, instead of watching it.

I have been dissociating during sex for as long as I can remember. When I was raped, my body had to conclude that whatever was happening didn't matter, which helped me to endure being violated. But it doesn't help when it comes to consensual sex. I value sexual intimacy and my sexuality, but, simultaneously, it doesn't matter to me. I can effortlessly zone out of whatever is happening so that I don't even notice when it is happening. I am a sexual person and value sexual connection deeply, and I also have the ability to have sex with anyone because, in an instant, I can make it not matter.

For a sexually violated person, accessing a healthy sexuality can feel like living on an edge between two halves, each one trying to pull you to its side. Until a few years ago, I played roles as mindlessly as starting my car, using sex as fake intimacy and unknowingly trading my body for attention and affection. Sex was a purely performative, man-focused act, during which I sidestepped my own feelings and boundaries to create space for the other. I was an 'escort' again, in everything but taking money. I had internalised male-centred sex as normal sex. If I'd had no escort experience, this would probably have remained mostly unchanged. Owing to the porn-saturated culture we have created, women cannot avoid internalising this to some degree.

Making sex all about men suited me because I never had to confront the part of me that needed to be cherished and was grieving this loss. When men were gentle with me and wanted to know more of me, it was confusing. I didn't know how to be. It didn't fit with what I knew. Being dominated and abused was where I felt the safety of familiarity and of knowing my role. This still shows up for me. I am still learning how to accept the right sort of attention from men. Sometimes I don't know the difference between good attention and bad. I worry I will be tricked again - worry that I'm tricking myself. I'm guarded, ready to defend. I will not be tricked again.

I dissociate during sex, but I also dissociate when my past triggers me in a certain way. It happens less often now. I may be talking or writing about some aspect of my experiences, and my body becomes rigid and freezes. I feel stunned. I swallow, cannot utter a word or a sound. This goes on for a few seconds, the enormity of it all too much to articulate. I touch the chair I'm sitting on. I feel the texture of my clothes. I look all around me. I breathe.

What do I know of men? I know of their sexual entitlement and of their aggression. I know of them mocking porn performers and single mothers. I know of them questioning rape victims, abandoning rape victims, outing rape victims in WhatsApp groups, remaining friends with rapists, starting 'revenge porn' web pages.

I know their fear when they say that feminism is man-hating or when they deny the oppression of females, in which all men are complicit.

I know of being cat-called while cycling to work, too many times to count. I know of fifty-year-old men offering me an extra fifty euro for anal sex. I know of my hair being pulled too hard. I know of their fingers pressing into me. I know of being sexually assaulted in my car. I know of hands in places they are not welcome, eyes looking me over, eye contact that feels like oppression.

I know of men wanting me in the same way they want food

– something to consume. I know of being smacked across the face so hard I thought I'd go blind. I know of teenage boys making mooing noises at me in a pub. I know of rapists who have careers in the public eye. I know middle-aged men who did not care about the inherent vulnerability of a twenty-three-year-old girl. I know of teenage boys following me home at night, shouting about blowjobs. I know of kerb crawlers looking me up and down from the safety of their cars. I know of 'You doing business?' being said to me by a passing stranger. I know of men who minimise sexual trauma to avoid feeling discomfort, and who label their ignorant opinions as 'free speech'. I know of men's comfort with feeling power over women.

I know of men who harshly judge women for selling sex but make excuses for the men who pay for it. I know the hyper-defensive reaction from many men when they try to argue with me about pornography. I know the nerves of sexual entitlement and fear that I touch off. I know friends who have defended paying their way inside women in foreign countries, who tell me I should keep my past a secret.

I know the hopelessness of male silence.

I know the ugly and barren centre of 'toxic masculinity' because, since I am a woman, I have had no choice but to dwell within it.

Although it is improving, it doesn't take much to be called

a 'man hater'. Simply referencing male violence without acknowledging that men can also be victims of abuse at the hands of women, can get you that label.

I am not a 'man hater'. I don't even know what it means to be one. I've never harmed a man. I've never hit or abused one, or cheated on one. I've never betrayed or raped a man. I've never sexually exploited a man. I've never tried to pay a man to have sex with me. I've never stalked a man, online or off, I've never threatened a man with violence. I've never harassed a man. I've never sexually assaulted a man. I've never rated a man's sexual skill online. I've never mocked a man's weight out of the window of my car as I drove past. I've never followed a man home. I've never gone into a space populated by men and opened fire. I've never formed organisations to teach other women how to manipulate men into submission. I've never written weird manifestos online about my hatred of men. I've only ever seen the men I know in good faith, sometimes too much so. I have every reason to hate men, as a class, but I don't, and I can't.

I sit in cafés and wonder which of the men around me buy sexual access or have bought it. Who has tightened their hand around a woman's throat, pulled her hair so much she couldn't breathe? Who among them has carefully considered how many stars to give in their review? I have to shake the thought that I am surrounded by punters, but it's hard to trust that you're not when you've seen how easy it is for them to move through the world undetected, just like most rapists do.

Young, middle-aged and old men pay to put their penises inside the bodies of eighteen-, nineteen-, twenty-year-old girls – sometimes younger. They have been raised in a patriarchal society saturated with the message that they are entitled to behave in this way. They have grown up with misogynistic cultural messaging and sexism in the workplace as a non-event or a joke.

They have been raised on harmful behaviour being laughed off or ignored. They have been raised seeing women doing the tedious domestic jobs – laundry, vacuuming, cooking, plodding around supermarkets and cleaning bathrooms. They have been raised hearing terms like *tramp, slut, bitch, hussy, whore, cunt, slag*. They have been raised with the message that women are to blame for men's predatory and violent behaviour. They have been raised to expect their name to be the only name associated with their family. They have been raised seeing mostly men in positions of power and authority – the implicit message that women are not entitled to power. They have been raised seeing credit given to men who do the bare minimum of parenting. They have been raised knowing that the Magdalene Laundries existed and seeing single mothers stigmatised and treated unjustly. They have been raised hearing about suspended rape sentences, on cat-calling being a joke, and on opinionated women being dismissed as 'hysterical' or 'emotional'. They have been raised on women being responsible for emotional peacekeeping and social and emotional labour, so they have never learned it themselves.

They never received the gift of being encouraged to connect with themselves, but instead along the way, received a sense of entitlement.

They have worked hard for their money, and they are going to get value for it, and, if not, they'll write on the review site about how the escort was older looking than her photographs. And all this time they have had free access to hardcore, misogynistic, violent pornography depicting women as submissive to men.

They wank to women being choked, spat on, smacked, punched, gagged, caged, whipped, exploited and tricked. They wank to women being hurt, to women being called sluts, whores, bitches and 'fuckmeat'. They wank to *facial abuse, anal abuse, abused schoolgirls, painful anal, teen abuse*. They wank to gang-bangs and *forced facials*. They pull porn moves on their sexual partners. They ejaculate to things they may not consider doing to a girlfriend or wife, not necessarily because of her feelings but because it would be too revelatory of their own.

The men who rape women, pay for sexual access, harass them on the street and in the pub, nag them into sex, creep on teenage girls on Instagram and register on sugar-daddy websites are men we all know. The same men who watch 'extreme rough teen anal humiliation' porn also watch their kids on sports day. Men who take their girlfriends on nice weekends away can also, every now and then, pay a twenty-year-old trafficked foreign woman with no English in a Sandyford apartment to swallow their semen. They are our managers, our colleagues, our neighbours, our local politicians, our sons, our fathers. They are lawmakers, bosses and men in leadership positions. They voted for equality and to repeal the eighth amendment. They wore the badge and had the sticker on their car, but they will never vote to repeal their sense of entitlement to a woman's body. They will never sacrifice their precious orgasms via a paid female body, whatever the cost to her.

They don't want liberation for women because that would be the end of their power-fuelled orgasms. And they will never talk about it because they *know* it is wrong. They know that it is a type of rape and that, therefore, they are a type of rapist.

There are thousands upon thousands more men who pay for sex than women who sell it. We know that the vast majority of women in the sex trade are there as a consequence of force, coercion, poverty, addiction and desperation. And for what? So a man can have an orgasm. What is the difference between these men and other men? These men have been so disconnected from their own humanity, and, therefore, can easily disconnect others from theirs. They have been dehumanised and, in dehumanising women, they further dehumanise themselves.

When we speak about sexuality, or anything that touches its edges, we focus on women and mostly ignore men. Women's sexuality is mysterious and forbidden. Men's sexuality is apparently basic and obvious and nothing remarkable. Nowhere is this more apparent than issues around the sex trade. Here, women are scandalous objects to be pored over and interrogated: *How did you get into it? Who was the worst punter? Were any of them violent? Were there any nice punters? What was it like?* We want to know all about her experience and perspective. After she has been physically violated, we want to violate her mind for the details. The men who have paid her are background artists. We take them and their misogyny for granted. There is nothing special about them because our standards for male behaviour are so low, and we have normalised male sexual entitlement to the extent that creeps are standard. There are about a thousand women involved in the sex trade in Ireland, and over a hundred thousand male punters. The imbalance of focus is striking, but also predictable.

According to the psychologist Nicholas Groth, there are three types of rapist.

The *anger rapist* rapes out of rage to humiliate and overpower his victim. He uses unnecessary physical force, brutality and profane language during the rape.

The *power rapist* feels inadequate as a person, and wants power and control over his victim. He tends not to use unnecessary violence. He is usually opportunistic, compulsive, and commits rape multiple times. He may be the most common type of rapist.

The *sadistic rapist* has eroticised pain. His rapes can be drawn out, involving torture and penetrating the victim with objects. He takes pleasure from the helplessness and pain of the victim and often targets women in prostitution or other women he sees as 'promiscuous'. These rapes may end in murder.

I encountered many men like this during my time in the

sex trade. They didn't have to hold me down to exact their gratification because the money and the sense that I was working were already doing that.

If the men who paid me weren't rapists, if this was all consensual sex, why am I traumatised by it? Why do I experience flashbacks with the same tone and texture as flashbacks I have had from being raped? I have had a lot of sex I regret having which I am not traumatised by. There is sometimes sadness, but not trauma. I experience trauma and flashbacks only in relation to sexual exploitation. Sex that didn't involve money, in which I've felt dissociated, or didn't feel like it, or when I didn't stop something I wasn't comfortable with has not traumatised me in the way sex-trade sex has – sex to which I 'consented'.

With distance and self-compassion, these men are alien to me. They can go to an apartment, hand over cash to the woman who answers the door, then remove her knickers and put themselves inside her. I find unfathomable the extraordinary and profound lack of compassion and internal disconnection needed to have an erection and push your penis into someone you know doesn't want it there, to have raped and not to care.

A therapist who worked with men who 'used' women in the sex trade told me that they feel in some way inadequate in their lives. What satisfaction is to be gained from paying someone to fake intimacy with you if there is no void inside you, if you have healthy self-esteem, if you are self-compassionate and compassionate towards others? If you are courageous in facing your own issues, inadequacies and distresses?

If we are healthy and attending to our own emotional needs, there is no room for control or domination in any type of relationship. Men who pay for sexual access need to go to therapy and confront their significant issues, heal their many hurts and take responsibility for them, instead of projecting them onto the vulnerable women in the sex trade. Prostitution is men forcing women to absorb their trauma.

I used to give talks to teenage boys about their role in preventing male violence against women. I still believe there is value in this work, but I think it has to come after something else. Carl Jung is believed to have said, 'The reason for evil in the world is that people are not able to tell their stories.' We must listen to people's stories, especially those of children, so that they don't end up attempting to compensate for not being heard or seen later in life. Just as I want to offer an alternative to women and girls, we must offer an alternative to boys and men to the rigid, disconnected, prescribed set of unspoken rules about how to relate to women. Teaching boys about consent is not enough and is not done early enough. Sometimes, it is more important to listen than to teach. Ignoring the indisputable impact that mainstream pornography has on the brains of boys and young men, does them, and the women they will encounter, an enormous disservice. Male sexuality is as complex as female sexuality and I believe that, by following certain gender norms, we are letting men down by ignoring their sensitivity, their fears and their yearning for connection.

A couple of days after I'd done a radio interview based on a TEDx talk about rape I'd delivered, I was leaning against my front door with a bowl of yoghurt watching my dog mooch around in the bushes. My neighbour popped out of his house with his kids. We said hi to each other. Then he says, 'Well done on the radio', while looking directly into my eyes, and I wanted to die. I wasn't expecting him to say anything to me, even if he did know about it or had heard it.

'Oh, thanks,' I said, laughing, as if talking on air to hundreds of thousands of people about being raped was hilarious.

'It must have been hard,' he said.

'Ha, ha, yeah, no, well, I'm used to it,' I said, just to get him to stop talking about it so openly. I wasn't used to it, especially from a man. I wasn't used to being trusted like that. I wasn't used to someone trusting *themselves* like that.

'Yeah, it's gotta be hard, though.'

'Well, thanks,' I said, and went back into the house with the dog.

Something shifted inside me. I felt the *It's okay* sensation. It *is* okay to be open about being raped. I felt supported in a sphere of life where too many men – and women – are afraid to show explicit acknowledgement or support because of their own awkwardness, discomfort or inadequacy. Recently I was collecting money for the Dublin Rape Crisis Centre, and a man brushed past me, making a weird show of avoiding me. His wife came behind him and said to me, 'Don't mind him. He's just embarrassed.' And I was left thinking, *Embarrassed about what?* And I wondered why I was expected to accommodate and excuse a man's embarrassment.

My neighbour saw and acknowledged me. He is a man, and he wasn't embarrassed and didn't avoid the topic or pretend he hadn't heard the interview or gloss over it. Because of this, I know I can trust him. And knowing there are trustworthy men in the world is a small balm. Courageous men soften some of the pain other men have lodged inside me.

In 2015, I helped my friend Grace to write a play called *The Game*, about men who pay for sex. It was part game-show, part re-enactment of true stories from the sex trade, and I wrote three of my own experiences for it. It required five new male volunteers every night to play the game-show contestants/punters and two female actors playing the game-show hosts/women. The men did workshops to prepare them for the hour on stage, but there was no script. They didn't know what was coming or what they'd be invited to do.

The first night I saw it, a man with huge stature and presence was taking part. During one scene, he was told to pick up a gun and threaten the female actor with it. He couldn't do it. He threw the gun down, 'tagged in' another volunteer and went off-stage, where he was supported by a therapeutic supervisor. A while later, he came back and took his seat with the other volunteers. One shuffled over and put his hand on the man's shoulder, and I felt my heart breaking open, a sob ratcheting up from the base of my throat. My heart wasn't opened by witnessing my stories of abuse being played out, but by what had been missing from all these moments: male heart, male tenderness and male courage.

The volunteers were courageous for that hour in the theatre, and I didn't have to be. I could just look after myself. By replacing the real men who inspired these stories, they helped to take away the punters' power and replaced it with their care, their gentleness, their love and their regular out-loud declaration that they were 'not that man'. They honoured me and they honoured my experiences. Most men do not pay for sex. There are far more men who are connected to themselves than there are who are so tragically disconnected. I hold this knowledge in the still splintered parts of my heart.

I am safe now. The guy in the play exists. I bring him up in my mind and feel my body respond. I breathe in the feeling. I am safe now. The man who shuffled over to comfort him exists. I am safe.

I cling to moments of male tenderness and tuck them into my heart to pull out when I feel hardened in the midst of more male violence against women, when I feel that the world is populated by evil. I saw the revelry among so many men when the players in the Belfast rugby rape trial of 2018 were all acquitted. I saw the defence of the players' attitudes and behaviour, and I felt ill and alone – and I felt a helplessness that was so raw, it turned me numb.

Days after the acquittal, I met a tearful woman at an impromptu protest rally outside the GPO in Dublin, who said her male colleagues were clapping in the office about the result. Clapping. My bones grew heavy with fatigue as I listened to her.

I see rapists being excused from custodial sentences because of good character references and their work record. And I see foreign women in prostitution being fined and convicted for their trauma while their pimps wait in the car outside the courtroom, while the men who paid to violate the women remain in the shadows, anonymous and unknown, and get away with it. Same as it ever was.

I am tired of seeing women in prostitution and pornography being shamed and judged by the same men who click into Pornhub at night. I am so tired of rape victims being viewed with suspicion and the accused being viewed with pity. It is exhausting being immersed in a world where violence against women is normalised, where rape is minimised, where paying for sex is still defended, joked about and encouraged, where we barely glance at the daily reports of men raping and abusing women.

I gave a speech at a rally a few weeks after the Belfast rugby rape trial concluded, in which I intended to include words about men being the solution to the problem of men's violence against women and girls. As I looked out at the several-thousand-strong crowd, I realised I had never seen so many men at an event like that before. They were moved to show up and declare their intolerance of other men's violence, and I became emotional as I looked at them, young, middle-aged and older. I crossed out that piece of my speech and replaced it with a thank you to the men there. In that moment after the trial, those moments of heartbreak and hopelessness, we didn't need more challenges. We didn't need a lecture. We needed to connect to our hearts and allow ourselves to mourn the loss.

It frustrates me that I am emotionally moved by the bare minimum of male action on this. We are so desperate to feel safe that every morsel is celebrated. My biggest concern, to borrow from Martin Luther King, is that what hinders women's steps towards safety from male violence lies not in rapists being unreformed, but in genuine, good men remaining silent about what their brothers are up to.

We like to think that things are separate, that the rapist is not the punter, that the domestic abuser and paedophile belong in separate camps. The workplace misogynists and cat-callers are in another box altogether. But they are not in separate boxes, they come from the same pond of male entitlement. They just express that entitlement to a greater or lesser extent, depending on the variables of their lives.

When we are dealing with a cultural phenomenon, we are dealing with attitudes and beliefs that directly influence behaviour, and these can all be changed, but men must change them. In the same way that all white people are responsible for ending racism, the solution of male violence against women lies within men. The response of 'not all men' fails to acknowledge that it is indeed 'yes, all men' who are responsible for male culture. All men have inherent unconscious sexist and misogynistic biases, just as all white people have inherent unconscious racism, and all straight people have inherent homophobia to some extent. And all men benefit in some way from patriarchal structures and attitudes, whether they explicitly know it or not.

It is now way past time for all men to get comfortable with some discomfort. Every man who stays quiet about the abuses his fellow man commits against women is complicit.

To create wider change, men have to be open to discovering and analysing their own biases and inherent misogyny. Getting off to a fifty-year-old man choking a nineteen-year-old girl in porn (90 per cent of porn depicts male violence against women), then tweeting your tips to help women feel safe in the streets by crossing the road is hypocritical.

Societal change is hard-won. Crossing the road is easy to do and easy to feel good about. Challenging your use of porn and what material gets you off is less easy, and no credit will be handed out, because the work of change is personal, intimate.

Peer influence is the greatest motivator for change. Abusive men don't care what women are saying or doing. They care what other men are saying and doing. We need it to replace the toxicity we are currently drowning in, and only non-abusive men can do that, as role models in their friendships, families, in their workplaces and organisations. They can change the culture by being explicit, blunt and direct about their zero tolerance of male violence against women. They can start lobbying groups and associations. Men can have influence with one breath, and take it away in the next. By showing up to a rally. Or not.

I believe that all men who pay for sexual access are sexual predators. At best, they are sexually entitled men; at worst, they are sadistic rapists. When people defend the men who pay for sex or casually theorise about the sex trade from a position of high privilege, my chest tightens to the point at which my vision tunnels, and my whole body flushes with sudden heat. Yet I am paralysed, listening, gauging the safety of saying something, gauging how retraumatising that exposure could be.

About two years after experiencing the last punter I visited, the violent one who tried to rape me, I drove back to his apartment on a Saturday night in the hope of seeing him. I decided to go at about one in the morning since it would be quiet then, and I might catch him on his way home from being out in town. That logic makes no sense now.

I thought that if I could talk to him, I could explain that what he did was bad, and he would understand, apologise and wouldn't do it again to another woman. Everything would be set right. I clung to the idea that there was goodness inside him, that it was a misunderstanding. Just as I had tried to persuade myself that the teenage rapist didn't mean to rape me, I tried to believe that this man just didn't understand that he was doing something wrong. I drove out to his apartment building, but couldn't find the right street. I drove around and around, getting more and more upset. I had invested a lot in this. Eventually, I pulled in somewhere and sat there for a couple of hours chain-smoking before driving home. I felt devastated. I wanted so badly to hear the words *I'm sorry*. In my naivety, I wanted him to realise the harm of his behaviour, for it to have been an accident, for him not to have meant it. I wanted so badly for him to be good underneath.

I do not forgive any of the men who chose to hurt me. We might as well get that out of the way. Only an apology opens up the option of forgiveness, and none of them are going to be apologising to me any time soon. I've had to work very hard to be angry at what men have done to me. I don't have to forgive them to find 'closure', even if that is what I'm looking for. And 'forgiving' them does nothing helpful for me. I don't feel sympathy towards these men, but I can dig deep enough to observe the parts of them that must be hurt or fearful or insecure, the parts that feel that abusing women would be a comfort. Men who are well and emotionally mature do not pay women for sexual access.

If I deny them their full humanity, then in a way I am

denying myself my own and, if I write them off, I am declaring a hopeless, unchangeable situation. I will not write off these men in the way they have written off women and the priceless worth of a woman's sexuality. Doing that is to subscribe to the 'monster myth', an expression coined by Tom Meagher, where men are either 'good' or they are evil monsters.

To write them off is to play into the patriarchy's game, with its own rules, stereotypes, low expectations and ideas about 'real men'. To write them off is to write off hope, because hope comes from knowing that people, places and societies can change: things can get better, and people can be held accountable for their behaviour. It doesn't mean I'm going to be best friends with a man who has paid for sexual access, but I acknowledge that nobody is just one thing. If we deny men who pay for sexual access their full humanity, we may as well resign ourselves to the status quo. However, punters will not hold themselves accountable. It is up to all of us not to be passive.

I will not write off these rapists. I will not meet their entitlement, distorted egos, sense of worthlessness and objectification with my own. I will resist with my entire being. I will breathe love in, breathe it out and make up for what these men put into the world. I will love myself radically and express myself unapologetically in response to their inability to love themselves. There is no need for revenge, because they have to live with the consequences of their actions. Until they reflect upon their behaviour and seek to be better people, they have to live inside their own inadequate, selfish souls.

At some point during my last summer as an escort, I met a punter I'm going to call Seán. He was thirty-three years old and built like a mountain. There was a different atmosphere about him compared to other punters. When I met him, I felt weirdly self-conscious, making a stupid joke about the dull brown carpet in his hotel room. He was easygoing, calm and didn't say much. It was like when you meet someone new, and you feel as if you already know them, and the knowing is easy. I felt less of my escort-self and more of my self-self. My sense of humour came out. We talked about where he was from and things like that. He used the name 'Seán' in his communication with me, and I asked what his real name was. 'Seán,' he said, looking surprised. He didn't rush me or immediately start doing things. He actually seemed to see me beyond what I was there for. I felt no internal tension, no edginess.

I don't really remember the sex. I can remember being on the bed, but that's all. It's the only appointment that I don't look back on with some regret. He asked me why I was doing it and, as usual, I made some horrific joke about loving sex. He said I was beautiful, which was kind, and that I must be a nymphomaniac, which was less touching.

We stayed in touch via email, and he told me he was addicted to porn and to renting escorts. He said he knew this was the case, but he couldn't stop. A couple of years later, he agreed to be in a radio documentary I was making in college, so we met again. He took a day off work and drove across the city to do it. He wasn't concerned about his anonymity in the radio studio, though no one knew who he was. I wore a flowery dress and felt like an idiot while I nervously waited for him to arrive. There was a strange delicacy about our coming together in this non-sex-trade, non-sex-related way.

I wanted to know more about his situation. There was something about him that set him apart from all the other punters I'd experienced, and I wanted to know what it was. We talked more about his addictions, about how he started punting in the first place: he had been on the way home from a night out when a friend suggested going to a brothel, and he was hooked. Years later, he saw an escort who was foreign, couldn't speak much English. She was obviously being abused and working under duress. He said he saw recent self-harm scars on her arms. He left without fulfilling the appointment, and this was the catalyst for him to move towards ending his punting 'hobby'. Most punters would have continued with the appointment. Seán was unusual. The difference between him and the others is that he was more connected to himself, which meant that he could connect with the people he came into contact with, which interrupted his ability to continue the disconnecting act of paying a woman to consent to sex with him.

Seán told me that he was in severe financial difficulties. He told me that paying for sex was changing his relationships. He said it made him lose any desire to try with 'normal' women. He said he would like to be in a relationship but didn't have the patience for it – 'it' being authentic connection, which takes time, effort, trust in yourself and the other person, as well as self-awareness. He wasn't self-pitying. He bore himself in a way I can acknowledge now as deeply courageous.

The non-judgemental space we created allowed me to tell him how I had become involved in the sex trade. I knew logically that one thing had led to another. Being raped had made me vulnerable and the man – J – paying me for his sexual gratification had implanted the idea of selling sex. But I hadn't yet acknowledged to myself the abusive and traumatic element of it.

Seán was taken aback by what I told him. My persona as a sex-loving escort had been very persuasive. He said he wouldn't have guessed that I'd had such a past. I suppose if you tell a lie that others want to believe, it is very easy for them to believe it. We talked more about my experiences of the sex trade, the type of men who came to me, my hatred of the sex-trade online culture, of reviews. We talked about his addiction. Eventually, our communication trickled out.

I feel a softness towards Seán, despite what he had done to women for so long. I wonder how a man who was so open with me, so connected to himself, could have 'hired' the number of women he had, and I wonder at the power of this addiction, and the power of the narrative to which sex-trade advocates contribute, which encourages the men to remain in denial about what they are doing.

When it comes to the concept of being intimately connected to someone, I recoil and my skin shivers. I have mean, unreasonable, protective thoughts towards myself, *No one would love you. You've been polluted. You are not like other people. You are dirty. You don't get to have love. You are not allowed it. Think of the things you were capable of doing.* I remind myself to let my thoughts pass by. I remind myself that my thoughts are not actually true.

I feel infected. I know I'm not, but it still feels true that men's toxicity has seeped into my veins and become part of me. And why would anyone want to be close to that?

When I feel lonely, I say to myself, *You were raped and you made it publicly known. Men will be afraid. They will care what their friends and family think. Men definitely don't want to have a baby with a former hooker. They don't want someone with a load of man baggage. Men want a woman to introduce to their mothers, not someone who has given blowjobs for cash.*

I use 'hooker' because it's mean. I reduce men and I reduce myself, because feeling that I'm worthy of being loved is dangerous.

It feels like standing before the entrance to a black cave, widening my eyes to see in the dark. I'm afraid to consider that I deserve love because, what if I'm wrong? I could only blame my own stupidity for thinking it might be possible. I could only blame myself for going into a pitch black cave. I have experienced a slow eroding of trust in men that has left me considering that perhaps being my own self-contained, self-sufficient person is the safest way to navigate life, and I'm very good at that.

Part of me knows this isn't true, knows that a fear part is trying to protect me. But it doesn't mean it's correct and, even if it is, so what? Why not find out? It's more important to have a meaningful life than to feel safe. Detaching from our internal experiences means watching the fear and the consequential thoughts without believing them or acting on them. It isn't easy: some parts just feel so much more right than others, and this is where we have to double down on our non-judgemental awareness practice. When we learn how to watch our thoughts, instead of getting sucked into them as being right or true, we have the space and freedom to make calm, free choices.

I remind myself, *I have known love. I have the evidence. I know that I can know love again.* I have spent the past few years trying to put my own needs and desires at the centre of my life, to furnish it with things I enjoy, to allow myself things I love. This is what 'being of service' actually is, finding what you love and giving it to the world. I allow myself to be gently pulled in the direction of what draws me to it. I trust the sense of being drawn. I say 'no' more often. I raised my fees. I ask for expenses. I stopped working for free. I breathe into a new way of relating to myself.

I make myself remember the last time I liked someone a few years ago. I remember how it felt. I remember how my heart was bursting open with an unbridled desire to connect. I remember not being afraid. I wasn't afraid.

Men hurt me because they chose to hurt me.

It wasn't about me.

There wasn't something innate about me that made men abuse and hurt me.

It wasn't what I was good at.

It wasn't part of my identity.

I am allowed to be loved.

I am not ruined.

I am not fragments of the past crudely put together into a girl shape, woman shape.

My skin is mine and it is perfect.

My insides are mine.

My body is my own.

I deserve love and deserve loving. I don't have to feel it

every second of the day to know that it is true. I am worthy of love because I am a human being.

What do I know of men? I know my friend Damo, who comes to every birthday celebration of his friends, regardless of how he's feeling or how hungover he is. I know my friend Fintan, who lives in the UK and sends me occasional supportive text messages, which prop me up to an extent he will never know. I know how my friend Ross gently helped me remove an abusive man from my home. I know Ross' immense stature and strength, and I know how he uses these things for building, for lifting his son, for cuddling my tiny dog into his chest.

I know the expanse of love I felt for my friend Kev as we swam together towards the yellow buoy at Seapoint beach. His enthusiastic explanation of why he was having only cold showers was hilarious and I laughed so much, I swallowed sea water.

I know how RTÉ presenter Ryan Tubridy assured me before an interview about being raped that he would guide me and would not go where I wasn't comfortable. 'I'll mind you,' he said, and I had to swallow the rising lump in my throat. I hadn't realised I needed minding, that it was okay for me to be minded.

I know transition-year boys speaking to me after

I give a talk. I know my older brother, the expert children's storyteller. I know my therapist, who expresses unconditional acceptance for every part of me, who gives me safe, patient attention, and has a steadiness that I can anchor myself to. I know my friend Thurlow's sensitivity and gentleness. I know how he supports my work. I know my friend Dave, who treks out from Baldoyle to go for walks with me and the dog, and for an unreasonable number of months listened to me going on and on about how weird I find having a body. I know my friend Tom, who carries light inside his burning heart despite the darkness that ruptured his life, and he shares it just by being himself, like a beacon, a lighthouse signalling safety.

I know my dad, who leaves chocolate or boxes of dishwasher tablets on my kitchen table when I'm out, who walks the dog for me when I'm away, who helped me pay for my new washing machine and looks after me, and says things like, 'It's nice to be with you', and doesn't expect anything in return. I know him, and I know his unconditional love. I know all these men's love.

I try to put men all together. Are they all my dad or Kev or Dave? Or are they all the old man who abused me for an hour? Or are they all like punters? I have to know. Are men safe? Are they unsafe? I don't know.

I once found a sense of safety and familiarity in violence and objectification, so how am I supposed to know what or who is safe? But I know how I felt swimming with Kev. I know how Damo's crap puns make me laugh. I know how relaxed I feel when I'm around Dave, as I explain my prickly relationship with my body. I know the sense of safety I absorb from my therapist. I know the jolt of excitement I feel when I see Ross' car pulling up outside my house. I know how I feel when Tom emails me. It's okay. These ones are okay. You're okay. It'll be okay.

Despair is the price one pays for self-awareness.
Look deeply into life, and you'll always find despair.

Irvin D. Yalom, *When Nietzsche Wept*

MY BODY

When I was small, I sometimes had moments of miniature existential realisation, a profound realisation of something impossible to put into words. It wasn't just the realisation that I was alive, that I existed, it was the realisation that I was myself. It never lessened in importance no matter how many times it happened. It never became normal. I remember racing into my mother's bathroom while she was busying herself in front of her mirror to inform her of the fact of my existence. 'I AM MYSELF!' I announced, animated, and not sure why.

She wasn't surprised or even bemused, cheerfully responding, 'Yes, you are!'

Still, today, I feel the same urgency to inform someone else of this profound truth, this exisential truth. These are my hands. These are my fingernails. This is my skin. This is, apparently, who I am.

My body is a real thing. It takes up space. It is five feet ten inches tall and it weighs about ten stone. It is thirty-six years old. It has long brown hair and two green eyes; the left one has fewer eyelashes than the right. There are two ears, two hands, two legs, a set of hips and a spine holding everything together, like scaffolding. There are slight stretch marks on my chest from where my breasts have grown and shrunk and changed.

I find existing within a body at best a ridiculous absurdity, at worst a cage of barbed wire, a place too painful to reside inside but impossible to escape.

My body is covered with skin. The skin never stops, even all the way inside the places that open up – mouth, throat, vagina, ears – all skin. When does the skin inside our mouths stop being skin and become something else? My skin spreads in colour, from the very pale, creamy peach of my neck, chest and belly to the pink of arms and hands to the red blotches on my knees and elbows to the white where the skin has died. Some of the skin has been pigmented by tattoo ink – arms, shoulders, back, stomach, chest, side.

There is scar tissue on my left eyebrow from running into a door aged seven, on the fourth finger of my left hand from a childhood incident with a pair of dumbbells, and there's a mystery scar on my left knee. There are new scars from minor surgery, and a thin white line across one thigh from an accident with a knife in 2009. The eyelid skin of my left eye is thicker than that of my right, noticeable when I'm tired or have a migraine. It makes my eye look weird.

It makes me not look like me. I don't recognise myself – or don't like what I do recognise. I wonder if I could be someone else on the days this happens. I wonder if all it takes to be someone else is to have one weird-looking eye.

I am most uncomfortable with skin. It is frustrating to feel this way because my skin is soft and smooth. Some parts are remarkably soft, and I stroke these places with one finger, willing myself to feel compassion towards them. I can't appreciate my skin because it is also where I have been touched, where I meet the world and where the world meets me. Where all the crimes against me are branded, on and into my skin. Harm has met my skin and could still meet it.

I regularly remind myself that my skin cells regenerate themselves every six weeks. This skin is not that skin. That skin has been washed and brushed and worn away. It has been flushed down plugholes, left in beds and clothes; it has been exfoliated off, creamed off, scraped off and pulled off. New skin has taken its place.

I wash my body in the shower. I look down it, the ridiculous lumps that are my breasts. Pale squashy lumps. I grip my stomach fat and look at it pushing out from between my fingers. I try to see my body objectively, as a useful thing. I tell myself, *Everyone else goes around draped in skin and has no problem with it. They don't even consider it. No one knows you're having these thoughts, these physical sensations.* I google 'how to get over having a body'. I view my body in the same way I view pieces of vacuum-packed chicken in a supermarket refrigerator, parts of the whole, resembling nothing of the once-whole feathered bird.

I focus on places where the bone is very near the surface of the skin. I feel no discomfort with my upper arms, where the bone is embedded deep within. But the jaw and skull and hip bones are sites of deep discomfort. Trauma lives in the bones, I believe, in the cells of our bones. It sits and it settles and it waits in the most inside place. It weighs down bones. Trauma's seepage into marrow is silent and invisible. There is a theory that it takes nine generations for it to leave the body. In one study using mice, two generations of mice pups became fearful when exposed to the scent of cherry blossom. Their grandparents had been exposed to the scent and simultaneously given a mild shock. The pups were born with more cherry-blossom-detecting neurons than other pups. We inherit trauma from our ancestors and, unless we resolve it, we pass it down to whomever follows. It is difficult to dig it out from inside bones. You have to be as considered and patient as an archaeologist.

I am most comfortable when contemplating my innards – things we cannot see – guts and organs, my heart, stomach, lungs. Blood and fluid. When I was a child, I used to slice my thumb with a sharp blade and pull the skin apart to see the inside. The raw pinkness, warning spots of seeping blood. I'd pick at the dead skin around my fingernails until it went too deep. (I often had plasters on the skin of several fingers at a time.) I liked to see the blood. I am alive. I can feel pain. I am a real person. I exist in the world. I am made of physical matter.

Apparently the body replaces itself with new cells every seven to ten years. My yoga teacher says 'in the fullness of time' a lot – 'In the fullness of time your arm will reach the ground', or whatever. I tell myself, *In the fullness of time no trace of the body I had then will exist.*

I ask my therapist what he thinks about having a body.

'You're okay with having a body?' I ask.

'Yeah,' he says. 'It's there in the background. I don't think about it much.'

I want to say, *I'd like that. I'd like it to be like that for me.* But I don't. Instead, shame courses through my bones. My hands are clasping my knees, bracing, and I feel like I'm five years old.

'I just want to be happy,' I say.

'I know,' he says.

He says 'skin' out loud, like a maniac. It guts me. It makes me shiver and squirm and want to disappear inside my body, evaporate. *Skin.* I want to take my skin off, like a jacket, push it into the bin and then fuck the bin out the window. Sometimes I want to rip it off.

My skin is covered with hair. I remove it from my legs, underarms and vulva every day. I don't like how it feels against my clothes. It makes me feel unclean, even though I know that this is not even slightly true. But I still feel it, the dirt of the day stuck to my hair and being carried with me, my dirt and other people's dirt and the world's dirt.

In an illogical contradiction, I obsessively look after the hair that grows out of my head. I love brushing it and touching it. I touch it often, wrap it around my fingers, drag them through it. I flip it around from one side of my neck to the other.

I run my fingers over my skin, cup my jaw and try to relocate myself inside this body. I open my eyes very wide to feel the skin of my eyelids stretch. I practise somatic mindfulness. I breathe. I sit with the sensations. Nothing makes it less weird to inhabit this body. It is a little like accidentally overhearing yourself as an echo on the phone or watching yourself, seeing a candid picture of yourself. I refuse to watch, refuse to listen. This is what I really look like. This is how I really sound. This is what I really am, and how can that be true if I don't recognise any part? My inner experience and what I see or hear of myself have so little to do with each other.

Sometimes, when I'm taking off my clothes, I regard my body in the mirror. I make myself look at it and will myself to appreciate it. I know how lucky I am to have all the parts I have. I have never experienced any sort of eating disorder or body-image problem, nearly inescapable issues as a woman. I know how lucky I am to have such a healthy body. Nothing really hurts or aches. I try to be grateful for it all. I let my eyes travel around my body, but my gratitude is hollow. The problem is not with how my body looks or works, the problem is my having to inhabit it.

I had minor surgery and had to wait for ages in the hospital corridor. I didn't have a book or my phone, so I was stuck with myself, watching nurses go by. It was roasting and I had a moment of gratitude for the green and white hospital gown I was in. It lay lightly against the downy fur on my arms. I scanned my awareness around the different experiences of the gown – how it left pockets of air in the places where it was crumpled up, how parts of it delicately landed on my skin again, so lightly I could barely feel it. I had a moment of deep appreciation for that hospital gown. I didn't want to take it off. I felt like I was beginning to learn the world again, all physicality feeling new.

I take the somatic therapist and author Peter Levine's advice to explore my body for places that feel safe, that feel okay to inhabit. I discovered that the little bones that stick out of my wrists feel okay to be inside. My hair feels okay to inhabit. My eyes feel safe to be inside and my eyelids. I make contact with these places by touching them gently. Over time, I discovered that I could feel the skin on the inside of my left forearm and enjoy how silky soft it is and not feel disgusted by the way the skin stretches around the muscles, tendons and bones inside. I feel the skin of my left forearm and indulge in this enjoyment.

I was throwing the ball for my small, fast dog in the grassy area beside my house on a summer day under a blue sky in 2018, and everything was fine. Then an image of a dark-haired, middle-aged punter, staring up at me with his cold, unseeing eyes, came before me. His empty eyes were like a stamp in my brain. The images of my experience with him thundered in one after another, like violent home invaders, ripping apart my present world. I could feel the texture of his penis on my lips, in my mouth.

I coughed and tried to blink away the image. I'd never experienced it as strongly as this before. All I was doing was playing with my dog on the grass. I hadn't been triggered by anything. It was just happening. I had dealt with these images before. Previously, I put this punter in a pair of novelty giant sunglasses to black out his dead eyes. I pulled a screen between him and me so he couldn't see me. I put him in a stupid hat, turned him into a joke. But those things did not move his face and eyes this time. This was like being punched, being winded. The images came so fast that there was no space to think. I could feel the same self-disgust and repulsion at thirty-four that I'd felt at twenty-one.

It was surreal, as if I was not really there, like this was the creation of someone else, and I'd get back to my own life at some point. I felt light, unattached. I tried to reconnect. I looked at the dog and the grass. I touched my clothes. I pulled my hood up over my head. I felt the furry tennis ball in my hand. I put a picture of a happy memory over the intrusive one: my Berlin boyfriend and me playing table tennis in a playground, my favourite memory from living there. But it did not dilute the image. It was shoving itself up like a wall behind my eyes.

I felt as if I was losing my mind. I picked up the dog, went inside and sat at my kitchen table. Tears slid down my face, and I sat in the hopelessness that I was still dealing with this memory, this man and his dead eyes, over ten years later.

On days like this when I'm hijacked by a memory, nothing matters, and that bleeds into feeling that *I* don't matter, and I think, *What is the point of anything? What is the point of my life? What is the point of me?* The worst memories are clear as crystal, sparkling in my mind: the details of the room, the smell, the textures. I cannot summon a memory my friends are trying to remind me of, but I can summon the entire experience of that man in less than a second. This memory comes and goes pretty regularly as I write this book. I resist it every time. I have yet to learn how to befriend it.

That evening, I meet friends for a pint. I force myself to try to be normal, but I feel totally out of it, disconnected and fake.

When an image or a memory comes, I hear a rushing sound in my head. It's a little like blood rushing, but it isn't that. For those few seconds, it's the only thing I experience. It is simultaneously a sound and a feeling. Sometimes it makes me feel I'm crazy. I used to think it was resistance to the memory or image, or a symptom of dissociation. Now I just experience it and don't try to decide what it is. It's a shoving sound, a pushing sound, like a rushing tide soaking a shoreline, a dark cloud making its way across my brain.

It seems ridiculous to have this normal body and feel so much discomfort. It feels like deep self-absorption, so I don't speak about it to anyone. So many people have such physical struggles and I am inside this healthy body, but I cannot sit in it with any sense of ease. I feel as if I exist above it, or that I'm floating all around it unable to come home to it, unable to come home to myself, the prickly toxicity that dwells inside my body. But if I cannot be open to these parts, I cannot be open to happiness, freedom, spontaneity. Living, but not really living, is like a living death.

I used to wake up and pretend to be dead for a few moments, to preserve neutral space of nothingness – of gorgeous, empty, uninterrupted space. I would lie in my bed unmoving and make my breathing slow as much as possible and stare wall-eyed at the ceiling. If I denied that day, maybe it wouldn't exist and this load would not have to land. Just for today. But that was impossible, of course. It was a slight reprieve, an attempt to escape. I filmed myself doing this, to trap it, to preserve it. Then I made still images – of me trying to preserve a still image, trying to become a still image. This artistic endeavour did not offer me any relief.

When your body has been the site of your debasement, it can be painful to have a body, let alone to feel safe in one. I want to take off my body, turn it inside out, bleach my bones, scrape men's residue out of the inside of my skin, like a cyst is scraped out.

I cover my mouth when I'm talking to my therapist. Sometimes I cover my whole face with my hair. How can he really take me seriously when he knows what my mouth has done? How can he not find it repulsive?

I did a workshop with the actor and movement director Bryan Burroughs. I did it to help me find a new relationship with my body. After one class, I asked him if he'd ever come across anyone with my problem before.

'It's not being self-conscious,' I said, making sure he knew, 'but having a body at all is painful.'

He was already nodding and saying, 'Yeah, all the time. Especially if there's a history of abuse.'

Then I realised he could probably guess that something had happened to me. It didn't matter how kind and gentle Bryan was. Now it was fifty thousand times more uncomfortable to be around him in my body than it was before we had that conversation, because my shame had been seen.

A few years ago, I finally agreed to get braces. My dentist was a young man with a Limerick accent. He was funny, and he made me feel like a normal person with a normal mouth. I hated being with him because this earnest man was going to be unwittingly touching places that no one should have to touch: the inside of my mouth. All the spit and fleshy pink. All I felt was shame. I knew this was illogical. He didn't know the things my mouth had done, and presumably most adults have given and received oral sex. He was aware of what mouths do. Maybe that was the problem.

It took him an hour and a half to fit the braces. It felt like scaffolding was being put up in my mouth, full of pointy barbs and sharp plastic. I ran my tongue over them and loved the feeling of it. I tentatively touched them with my fingertips, as if I might make them fall off. Afterwards, the dentist wanted to show me something on the screen of how my teeth would look in a few months, but I didn't care. I wanted to leave so I could be alone with my mouth. I was already feeling protective of it. I was enjoying the feeling of the alien objects in it, I was nearly joyous. I went out to my car and took a photo of them to send to a friend. In the photo, I'm grinning my head off.

I minded the braces really well. I brushed them often and drank coffee through metal straws, so I didn't stain them too badly. I learned what to eat. I learned really quickly what not to eat. Sometimes it was hard to speak, but it was usually okay, and I don't do a lot of talking anyway. I read a poem at a workshop and had a lisp and felt like a teenager.

I wanted to tell everyone about my braces. I wanted everyone to see them. Whichever way my mouth organised itself around the braces gave it a slightly new shape. My lips had a new little turn-up on either side, like a dolphin smile, so even the outside of my mouth was new. In the pub, my friend Eoin told me that he might have to get some teeth removed. We discussed teeth and braces and mouths for a few minutes and I didn't want to die. He showed me a photo of a baby's skull, teeth all piled up waiting to drop down. 'Rotten, isn't it?' he said, but I was not repulsed. I was amazed. I had a brand-new relationship with my mouth, and I was so happy I could have exploded. My dentist had no idea of what he had inadvertently facilitated.

My body's nervous system has endured hundreds of unwanted sexual acts. My body has absorbed these acts and, whether I consented to them or not, the imprints have been made on my nervous system. My body learned not to protest because it would not be listened to, just as a neglected child learns there's no point in crying and goes mute. Our nervous system is so sensitive in the area of our genitals that even a gynaecological examination done without sensitivity or care can leave a traumatic imprint. If you have ever left your gynaecologist's clinic feeling emotional or shaky, this may be why.

Post-traumatic stress is an unfinished response to an earlier threat. If, after a traumatic event, we don't experience our feelings, if we don't get the chance to cry and shake, if our trauma is not seen and validated by another person, our bodies cannot discharge the energy aroused during the trauma. This response – fight, flight, freeze or fawn – remains clogged in our nervous systems, creating an internal map. The freeze response, the one closest to death, is the most common nervous-system response to sexual violence. The body instinctively feels that there is a threat to life and it collapses, like an animal does.

If we don't find a way into our bodies again after trauma, if we don't have our trauma validated, we can remain 'stuck' in the freeze response. When in that state, endorphins are released that numb pain, and so our pain tolerance threshold is raised. We are then physiologically able to endure further abuse; we are primed for it.

People with this system might find themselves stunned when faced with a trigger, unable to speak or take action. When we are triggered, our nervous systems immediately go into whatever threat response that has been mapped onto them. You can freeze when your neighbour shouts at you over a parking spot in the same way as you froze when you were getting raped. If we have endured repeated trauma from which there was no apparent escape, our nervous systems can 'flop', become passive and acquiesce to the abuse. Our response to triggers says nothing about who we are as a person: it is not something we can control. The response is always our nervous system's best idea for safety.

I get migraines on average once or twice a week. I've had them for more than twenty years, but they've become much more intense and persistent in the past few years, since I started writing this book. They knock me out of ordinary life. The medication knocks me out further, making me drowsy and foggy-headed. Migraines stop me being able to work, read, write, walk the dog, see friends, go to the supermarket. I often feel as if I'm broken or some sort of failure when they happen. I blame myself for not eating or for drinking alcohol, for not getting enough sleep or for letting myself get stressed. They also happen with no apparent trigger. The pain wakes me up, and my plans for the days ahead crumble.

The pain is like a screwdriver turning slowly behind my right eye. I have fantasised about scooping my eye out with a spoon. I've banged my head against walls in frustration with the pain. I've bashed the side of my head with the heel of my palm, which gives me a split second of nothing. Unsurprisingly, it always makes the migraine worse. I have drunk a whole bottle of wine, knowing that it would hurt me more later but it was worth it for the temporary numbing. I don't even bother telling my friends I have a migraine, unless it is a particularly bad one, since it is so normal for me and it feels so boring to report it over and over.

The pain isolates me from the rest of the world, dragging me into myself and cutting me off from spontaneous life and any sort of human engagement. I usually become depressed, as each task, even texting a friend, feels like a mountain to scale. If the medication doesn't work, I'm forced to be with it and all the feelings of self-blame that show up inside me. Like so many chronic conditions, migraine is private, unwitnessed pain. Nobody sees what it's like to be in the hardest places of an attack. Nobody sees the depression or the self-hate that comes up, the vitriol I experience for my broken brain.

A couple of years ago, I realised I needed to explore more options than medication. Migraine is a nervous-system disorder, and our nervous system is where we hold and process all of our trauma. Migraine is one of the commonest disorders of the nervous system and also one of the commonest symptoms of trauma, along with a low immune system, adrenal fatigue and fibromyalgia. I realised I just had to accept it as part of my life, instead of holding out for a day when it would be gone for ever. Getting to the point where you accept migraine with self-compassion is a journey in itself. It involves allowing yourself to slow down to meet the migraine, integrating it into your life and being, making space for the pain and not judging the self-blame that shows up, instead of forcing normal life to continue and struggling to endure it.

I discovered a man called Conor with huge brown eyes who does craniosacral therapy and acupuncture. Craniosacral therapy involves a light touch on different parts of your body. I didn't know anything about it, but I heard it could help, so I went to meet him. I told him all about my migraines, and that I had experienced a lot of sexual trauma.

As Conor came near me, I felt my body involuntarily squishing itself down into the table I was lying on, as if it could get farther away from him if it really tried. As he worked, I noticed my body freezing in different places, especially my lower body, and my breath becoming shallow. Afterwards, I felt shaky and exhausted. Then I had a three-week break between migraines – a previously unimaginable reprieve.

During another session, Conor had his hand at the top of my chest near my clavicle. He asked me beforehand to tell him how my body responded and if I wanted him to pause or stop. I didn't like it. I felt like I was trapped under his hand. I shut my eyes and batted away the feeling. I told myself that Conor was safe. But he noticed the discomfort in my body and stopped, and I felt embarrassed that I could endure abuse but not this gentle healing. I told him I didn't say anything because I knew it was safe, he wasn't going to hurt me. I wanted my body to realise this, relax and be cured.

He said, 'But if the body is saying, "Enough. This doesn't feel safe" or "This is overwhelming", we respect that, and move somewhere else.'

I felt so sad that I'd let my body down again, just like the other hundreds of times I'd ignored what it was trying to tell me. I still wasn't respecting it. This was such an insight into my relationship with my body. I had so much more to learn about it. No matter what the context is, it is possible to listen to it when it says no or too much or not now, and reconnect to myself. The resolving of trauma is not so much about telling the stories of what happened. It is more about gently guiding the body into the present and acknowledging when it doesn't feel safe. We don't need to make our bodies endure things in the name of healing. Healing is actually respecting our body's needs and slowly creating space for it to have new experiences, with patience and compassion, giving it the trust it wasn't granted before.

The nervous system has to build capacity to feel safe, and this does not happen quickly. It needs to feel alive, to feel pleasure, connection and goodness, in small, safe doses. We can do that by swimming in the sea, being mindful in breathing, or tasting food. We can do it with a healing touch or with hugs or holding a pet. We can do it by sitting and noticing ourselves. We can do it by making mindful movements with our breath, like yoga. For a traumatised nervous system, being present can feel threatening, but we can pendulate between being present and being dissociated or otherwise activated, with patience and compassion, increasing our flexibility and building our capacity to feel safeness in safety. The wonderful thing about our bodies is that if trauma can be passed through generations, so can healing and safeness.

My womb sits uneasily inside me above my vagina, which also sits uneasily inside me. The part of me that makes me a woman is the place where I have been attacked and violated.

It is also where I have been loved and cared for. The part of me that makes me a woman is the site of violence and the site of my rehabilitation. It is where evil has left its residue and where potential pure, new life could grow. The part of me where I give and receive love is also the part of me that draws misogyny and violence – the places of me that were meant for love and were filled with hate.

I would like to have a baby. Saying that makes me feel as if I'm transgressing against my feminist principles of not needing to acquiesce to what society expects to be inevitable for every woman, but I want a baby anyway. It's an uncontrollable, unchosen, internal want. Part of me doesn't particularly want a baby – the part of me that wants to attend to my own life and knows how easily I can erase myself to create space for others. Saying I would like to have a baby is also a monumental step of vulnerability, even though it's something most people want. As I write this, I am aware of the clock ticking inside me, and am deeply aware that I need another person to create the baby.

Once I admitted to myself that I wanted a baby, shame surged through me with an intensity I hadn't experienced before. I simultaneously decided that my womb and my entire reproductive organs are a dangerous place for a baby to grow in. I see pregnant women – women I don't know, and upon whom I can freely project impossible and improbable schemas of purity and wholesomeness – and think I shouldn't be near them. I unconsciously move away, as though my presence might infect them and the pure untouched thing they carry inside them. I feel an irritating sense of inadequacy.

The inside of *my* body feels like a toxic environment for a baby to develop in. If I get pregnant, the baby could feel the evil poison its mother has been infected with. It wouldn't be able to trust me. How could anyone trust me after the things I've done, the things I have allowed be done to me and the secrets I've kept? Surely a baby needs to trust the body it's growing inside. And my body let me down. If I couldn't keep myself safe, how can I keep another life safe? All those unpleasant and abusive men have left their stagnant, corrupting, toxic energy inside me, and any baby who tries to grow in my womb will feel scared and unsafe. And when the time comes for me to give birth, the baby will have to travel through the same place where I have been violated. It would have to touch the same skin the men have touched.

I decide that this is the absolute truth and I am devastated.

I would like a baby to grow in this body.

I let it out to C about the infected-womb thing and I want to disappear. I can't look at him, this womb-less man.

He says, 'I think you'd be a very loving mother.'

I think I might die. I want to disappear inside a huge black bin bag or turn into a cloud. I hate him for shining all this corrosive light on my most tightly held fears. I hate it but I keep showing up because he reflects parts of myself I tentatively believe are there, so I love him really. No one has ever said that to me before. I wait until it has passed. What he has said is too fragile to be aired now, to be seen, to be handled just yet.

Later in the week, his words keep popping into my head, and each time I feel my mouth form a smile. It was as if he had granted me permission. I had never considered this before. I usually smothered any thought of motherhood, too painful to examine. I was just sure about the truth of my body's apparent toxicity.

You need courage to be a mother and you need quadruple courage to be a mother when you have experienced sexual abuse, when your self-trust and world trust have been ripped apart. I replay C's words in my head. It's as though a window blind has been pulled up and a shaft of light is shining on the thing I lost, and I can see it. Some door in my heart opens up to another place. I might be wrong about a few things. Maybe I'm not doomed to repeat trauma indefinitely for the rest of my life. Maybe I would be okay. If my therapist – who sees all my weird parts – and my friends think I could be a good mother, perhaps it isn't true that my insides are infected with the evil residue of certain men. Maybe having a baby would be the purest, most self-loving and detoxifying thing I could do with my body, with the core of what makes me a woman. I remember that when I was being loved, I never felt this way about my insides.

I spent my twenties hating my period. My body was an absolute mystery to me. I never really knew when my period was going to arrive. It got in the way of life. It ruined clothes, trips away and sex, and caused me pain, all of which I resented. I feel a weird want for it now. I even sort of look forward to it, the low dull throb in my abdomen. I wallow in it, in the fatigue, in the lower back ache, the feeling of being drained, of being pulled down into the ground. My body is naturally itself. I have no control over it. It is beyond my authority, pulled by the moon. I know so little about my body that I can't really make decisions for it. It exists naturally, separate from my mind, and separate from concepts. Each month brings me a reminder that a baby is possible, despite what I think of myself, my reproductive organs or my ability to be a good mother. My body is doing what it is supposed to, despite all my beliefs about it.

There is no evil inside me. There is no pollution. The fact that my body remembers things that have happened to it does not make it a site of dirt and infection. The shame belongs with the men, not with my womb. My insides want to grow a new life, and they're allowed to. All my insides needed was to have the pain acknowledged about the hurt that was done to them. I lie on my yoga mat and consider my womb, my vagina, my entire reproductive system. I don't know how to start this new relationship. I put my hands over my lower abdomen and say to it, 'It wasn't your fault.' I tell it, 'I will do my very best to let you grow a life.' I breathe in and I breathe out.

Yoga means 'to unite'. It is the practice of uniting the body, mind and spirit, connecting us to our internal world, the wise core at our centre, and to each other. In the Yoga shala, I crouch into a squat and my elbows push my knees out, and I feel the gentle stretch. I breathe into the ache, breathe into the tightness, imagine it melting, flowing down my thighs and up my sides. The physical limb of yoga is one of eight parts, which include breath control, or pranayama, and meditation. It is an active process of engagement with the present, inviting us to access stillness within ourselves. It invites us to observe what is underneath, where all the answers are.

Yoga has helped me to develop a new relationship with my body. It has helped me access and trust my body's wisdom. It has eased me into self-acceptance, self-worth. Because the thing about practising the 'asana' limb of yoga is that it isn't primarily about becoming stronger or more flexible; at its core it is about acceptance and surrender with every breath.

Many aspects of yoga and psychotherapy feel to me like similar paths. We meet our private internal world on the mat; we cannot escape what shows up for us – comparisons, impatience, shame, insecurity. What we struggle with on the mat we struggle with off the mat. What shows up in the therapy room shows up outside it. Both are paths of present awareness, acceptance and self-compassion. Both teach us how to meet and notice, without judging, our thoughts, feelings and sensations. We learn how to soothe ourselves with the breath, how to slow down body and mind, how to cultivate stillness, even if only for a millisecond. We learn how to turn towards our experience and breathe it in. We learn to dissolve attachment to outcome or aspiration; we experience the safety and consistency of ritual – the ritual of an early-morning yoga class, of driving to the therapy room, of sitting every day at the same time for just fifteen minutes' meditation. We slowly ease into being with ourselves, however we are, from moment to moment, unattached to any of it.

My teacher assists during the classes, firm pressure here and there, a pull or a stabilising leg pressing against mine, and I am open to this, my body knowing it is safe. I am held safely by another human being. It is safe for my body to be held in all these weird ways. I say thank you to him every time. Not 'Thank you for gently shoving me deeper into the pose', but 'Thank you for the safe touch. Thank you for supporting me.' For nearly a decade, I have starved my body of safe touch, for fear it will become unsafe.

Yoga brings me home to my body, into the nature of myself. I exist from the inside out. Inside myself is the safe centre with which I meet life's events. My body is a naturally occurring thing, just as entitled to its place in the world as a tree or a jellyfish. The spiritual teacher Ram Dass said he tried to turn people into trees. We don't evaluate or compare trees, we just see them and appreciate them for what they are. 'You don't get all emotional about it,' he said. 'You just allow it.'

I swim in the sea, and the cold takes my breath away. For a moment, my body feels as if it's going into shock. But after three deep breaths, I can feel things other than the cold. I feel the water holding me up. I feel it smacking against my face, the wet in my hair, my limbs moving slowly through it. I feel my body in one place, and I am inside it. I am it and I am me, and I am the sea as well, and I am alive. I am euphoric and do big smiles at the other swimmers, wave at my dog tied up at the bikes, anxiously looking on. I feel the deep, soul-filling satisfaction that nourishing things give you, like when I notice that a plant has sprouted something new or when I'm experiencing a moment of joy with my friends. It feels so safe here that I don't want to get out of the water. I turn on my back and float along, listening to the sounds around me. *Let the sun warm up your skin*, I tell myself. *Turn your body out towards the sun.*

The quieter you become, the more you can hear.

Ram Dass

SURRENDERING

For my words to be made public, I have to build a steel heart out of the soft lump that pumps in the centre of my body. I don't know how to do that. I used to like to make birdhouses, paint them pastel colours and hang them on the ivy-covered trellis that clings to my back garden wall. With a sudden sense of urgency to make another, I poke around the shed, full of cobwebs, tools, gardening gloves and hanging baskets all sitting inside one another, in the hope that I might find some leftover wood. I find three bits, not enough. I take them out anyway and put them on my garden table. At least I've made a start. I regard them. This is what I'm doing with the insides I need to build. I'm looking at what I have and they're coming up short. I have to take these pieces and make them work.

For many of us who are overly self-reliant, the urge to protect others from discomfort, and therefore our own discomfort, is ingrained in our nervous systems. How much of ourselves have we erased to protect others and guard the peace? We can't protect people at the expense of who we are. Other people's feelings are theirs; we have to trust them to be able to look after themselves. We have to let their reactions be their challenges, their work. We have to feel free to talk about our shameful, murky things, whatever they are, or they'll never be resolved. We have to drag the truth of our lives into the light and love ourselves throughout the process.

It is okay to be the centre of chaos. It is okay to be the very source of the problem. I can be the source of the problem and cause people to feel terrible. I can be compassionate towards myself and towards them during it. It is okay to be the thing causing the ripples and also the tidal waves. Discomfort is okay. Pain is okay. Feeling hurt is okay. I feel the regular rise and fall of shame within me. It is also true that I am not ashamed of any part of what I did. I am not ashamed of any part of who I am. My two worlds – one known, one unknown – are coming closer and the crash will happen soon. I must be ready for it. There will be no returning to the safe in-between space. Many of the rooted parts of my life will uproot.

I cling to those who are supporting me as I'm writing this book. I ache with loneliness. The inside of myself feels barren and made of dust. I don't know how to become ready, apart from centring myself in genuine, loving awareness of whatever shows up in me and in others. I think that is all I need to do.

One day I say to C that when the book is done I think I'll feel free. The zest of freedom ripples under my skin, and I let it vibrate there, guiding me, as if I'm divining water. I read a quote from Jackson Pollock: 'The work has a life of its own. I try to let it come through.' I am a vehicle for my stories, my writing, whatever I experience. I am not *the* story. Freedom is letting whatever is coming up from within us to move through us. I am that through which experiences move. I am not the experiences. The integrity of the sky is not harmed by the passing of rain clouds.

All this actually happened, I say to myself. This was a part of my life. This did happen. I am amazed. I am speechless, unable to get my head around it. I was sexually exploited. It happened. I have to repeat this to myself to believe it. I let the part of me that knows this truth speak to the part of me that is afraid. It's okay. I was sexually exploited. Everything I have written about sounds very dramatic, but it doesn't feel dramatic. I don't look back and feel drama. I look back and feel the unnecessary pain that trickled through my life as a consequence. I look back and see how I have wasted so much of myself. How boring it all was. How jaded and oppressive it feels to play within the system of patriarchy, compared to how my heart ignites at the thought of its upending.

Some days, I think I should stop writing this. A sense of certainty rises inside me, like a tight, silent scream, blistering out to the edges of my body. I sit in a stupefied, stunned silence in my garden, regretting the waste of time this past year and a half has been. I have had many conversations with my friend Riadhna about the pros and cons of writing my book. My hopes and fears. I weigh them up. I try to foresee the many negative consequences. I try to figure out the best option for me, and I get lost in anxiety. I tell myself that I've been through enough, that I'm owed something that feels good now, to write something else that would more likely grant me validation from others – all those things writers want.

On other days, I'm sure again that it is the right thing to do. Remembering how meaningless and uncertain everything is does help. That when I die, I will not be thinking about how I should have written something else. I let go of having to know if it's the 'right' or 'wrong' thing for me. I let go of my attachment to it as something that means something about me. My mind tries to protect me from harm, but I don't need protection.

Most crucially, I am ignited to detach from my ego when I reflect on courageous people who have spoken out about the truth of their lives despite the consequences. I owe it to them, and I owe it to all who come after me. There is a reason this has been pulling at me to write, turning me over and over through the pages for eight years now. It is time for me to tell the truth of who I am.

Being courageous for the good of something bigger frees me from the limitations of personal self-doubt and the shame of being seen, because it is no longer about me or my feelings. It becomes an act of service. It was never a choice. It feels like a pull, like falling in love, a burning inside, a dragging along, part of the natural order of things. You can't really choose it. You just have to surrender and let it happen, surrender to the work coming through you.

Holding a secret close to you can be as crippling as what happened to you. You negotiate the world while holding all the parts of yourself together, bracing, not trusting, always censoring in case something leaks out, unable to claim your entire life as your own. Not speaking about my past was protective, for sure, but cutting off my past was cutting off a part of myself. It is lonely. It goes beyond sexual violence or the sex trade: I could be writing about any part of myself that I am keeping secret. Liberation is the slow, painstaking integration and acceptance of the story and all your parts, with support, if you're lucky. We all have secret parts of ourselves that are private and intimate and only for us to experience, layers and layers of unknown. It is so impossible to know someone else's layers, and even our own layers can often be secret to ourselves. We all have things nobody is ever going to know about. We all have secret lives. Everybody has a story.

Every time I tell the story, it gets a little lighter to carry. Every time I tell the story to a trusted friend and nothing changes in the relationship, the world gets safer. My dog loves me and my god-daughter loves me. She loves me because of who I am – who I actually am – despite what I feel I am under my skin. She has no history upon which to create a schema around me, her knowing of me is the purest knowing, despite what I sometimes feel I am under my skin. I go over to her house and play with her. I pull her onto my knee and bury my face in her soft blonde hair and get two seconds of her before she struggles away. She is five and will not acquiesce to a hug she doesn't want. I love her so much that sometimes I can feel an actual pain in my chest. I want to protect her from the pornified world we have created. I am doing my best for her and for her sister, for me and younger me, and for my future children and all children. Little boys don't deserve to be conditioned to feel entitled to objectify a woman's body. And little girls don't deserve to be conditioned to feel they have to swallow and accommodate that entitlement.

Whatever happened to you or whatever weird things you have done, I am with you. In the times you feel you can't stand it any more – whatever 'it' is – I am with you. We give ourselves a hard time for our choices from an adult lens that has long forgotten what it is to be young and naive and inexperienced. It's easy to look back at the times when we feel we let ourselves down or disrespected ourselves, let our dignity be taken from us, and be frustrated with ourselves, but we were doing the best we could to meet our needs with the awareness we had then. Just because we have more awareness now doesn't mean we 'should' have had it before. It doesn't mean we were stupid. You can be compassionate to those parts of yourself that are still hurting. You can say, 'It's okay, I'm here for you, I'll mind you.' You can mind your younger self. Hand yourself the gift of sweeping forgiveness.

There is no need to pick through everything, examining which parts are forgivable and which aren't. Forgive it all in one go. Forgive yourself for how you responded to men who wanted to hurt you. Forgive yourself for pandering to their egos. Forgive yourself for being human. Inhale, and be aware of all the people around the world who struggle with self-judgement. Know that you are not alone. Exhale forgiveness for yourself and for all others, one broad brushstroke of radical forgiveness. If you aren't allowing yourself to feel what you feel and know what you know, this will show up for you later. Trust what you're feeling, and trust what you know. And if you don't know what to do, do nothing and surrender to stillness. Allow it to reveal your inherent wisdom.

I used to want to be anything other than who I actually am because I didn't know who that was. I wanted a box I could put myself into where I knew what my role would be – a rape victim, an escort, a rape survivor, a sex-trade survivor, a sexual-exploitation survivor, a domestic-abuse support worker, a rape activist, a sexual-exploitation activist, a trauma therapist. All these meaningless identities. I like performing as an art form but, in daily life, I found that performing without a script was quite difficult. If we buy into the idea that we must identify as something, we remain trapped in this place, always holding ourselves in judgement as to whether or not we are doing the identity well enough in the eyes of others.

I wanted to put this trauma into anything I could, to take the spotlight off the pain and shame, and turn myself into someone who could contribute – turn the spotlight on that instead. I thought this was 'doing recovery'. I thought if I could just keep doing things to prove I was a person of value, I would eventually believe it, and I would be okay. So I completed three degrees, trying to find a place where I could prove my worth and be of service most efficiently. I thought I was beyond healing, but my role was to prevent and help heal the harm men cause. But if we have to prove something, we are tethered to whomever or whatever we have deemed to be the judge of that proof. We cannot live freely from one moment to the next if we are playing to an imaginary jury. Role-playing and living up to perceived expectation eventually crushes us because the pain of not expressing ourselves outweighs the comfort of staying hidden.

When I take away the need to play a role, I am freely doing what my heart draws me to do, the work I am here to do. If you can create a little stillness, your *dharma* – the work you are on the earth to do – will find you. If we need to have a purpose, I think this is it, to let your heart draw you to things, even if it causes some discomfort in yourself or others. To put yourself at the centre of your life and enjoy it and not to have to prove yourself worthy of it. Especially if you have been profoundly hurt.

Despite the pain in your heart and despite the pain all around you, give yourself permission to enjoy your life. Make your only task in life be to enjoy it. This might be the real 'healing', for you, for everyone around you and for the world at large.

When I was in first class, aged six, we had an older girl minding us for a couple of hours. It was Christmas time, and we were making cards. The minder asked for people to sing carols. I sat there with my paper and crayons, wanting to sing a carol so badly, it physically ached. But I was paralysed and stayed quiet and another girl sang a carol while I burned with jealousy, telling my six-year-old self that I didn't really want to sing a carol, dousing the burning embers I had inside me before they had a chance to set fire to anything. I was so terrified of being seen as wanting something. It was too vulnerable. It was too shameful.

I have experienced many other *petites morts*, when I have smothered a part of myself that is trying to express itself. It's the part that lets people talk over me. The part that spent ten years writing poems but not reciting them to anyone. The part that decides that the things I want are for others, not me. The part that fawns. The part that mutes itself in the face of aggression and disrespect. The part that waits and sees, instead of going in and declaring. The part that didn't leave the room. The part that bends to accommodate 'reasonable' arguments. The part that didn't report rape or sexual assaults. The part that was stunted and silenced and paralysed when the flash from a camera on a tripod went off again and again. The little things are as big as the big things because they all come from the same place. They all come from muting myself, erasing myself. But a small death is also an opportunity for a small renewal. When something dies, another thing inside us changes: we are transformed, we adjust to a new life with the loss. The change may be unwelcome and difficult, but if we can embrace it, transformation can happen.

I know this book may not be welcomed by some sections of society. That's okay. I still need to say my things that need saying. Voicing your truth is a gift to everyone who hears it, whether they agree or not. It gives permission to others to speak their truth too, especially if it's hard to say. It is especially a gift then. When we speak from our hearts, we speak to the hearts in others, and we allow others to feel safer in speaking from their hearts too. If we don't draw our own lines, others will feel free to violate us. If we don't expose the wrong, the wrong-doers will not expose themselves. If we pander or adjust to systems, the systems are maintained. If I allow my courage to sit in silence, it is not going to inspire anybody else to use theirs. It is not going to change anything, or challenge anything or influence anything.

I still feel weird about existing inside a body, but I profoundly appreciate the warm air grazing over the hair on my arm. I close my eyes and hold out my hands, facing the breeze on the beach and feel it moving between my fingers. I feel gratitude to be able to be in this place. I feel grateful for the small weight of my dog in my arms. I feel grateful for the yellow of sunflowers, grateful to witness my god-daughter and her sister in their paddling pool, grateful for the existence of whales and all cetaceans, grateful that a stray cat and her four kittens chose my parents' shed to nest in.

I've learned that being grateful is a mature feeling. I deserve and am grateful for the gifts that others bring into my life: their presence, text messages, invitations, reminders that I am normal, I am ordinary. I feel a surge of 'less than' and let it pass. I have mined valuable jewels from travelling through the underbelly of our human existence, inside the shadow part we all carry within us. There is no blame and there is no judgement. There just is: the feelings, the thoughts, whatever. We can flow with these tides of feelings, knowing that for every wave coming in, there's a wave going out. The only thing that is real is this moment – observing ourselves.

The things men did to me belong to them, not to me, not to my body. When I'm walking the dog, when I'm unloading the dishwasher, when I'm sweeping gravel off my path, I tell myself, *You are doing your best*. I clean up the garden, gaze at the flowers and all my garden decorations, and am overcome with feeling pathetic, full of dirt again. I want to destroy it all. It would be so satisfying to pull everything out of the ground. It would be such a weird, sad relief. I resist, and tell myself, *You deserve these flowers. You're allowed to like your flowers. You're allowed to collect garden decorations.* These times come and go. Feeling great comes and goes. I don't know where I am with it all now, except that it's a bit easier for me to be present than it ever has been before. And I'm aware that there is much to get out of being present to ordinary moments. I am more connected to myself than I have ever been. I have the ability to hold the ache and the gratitude and the lightness and know they can exist together because they are part of me. I don't have any solutions to offer because I am not sure I'm presenting a problem. My friend Grace said to me, 'Love is the answer to the difficult questions.' I'll try to be love – love for myself, love for others, love for my 'enemies', love for the world, especially when it is hard to love others or the parts of ourselves we need to love most. We're not here to worry about whether people love us or not. We're here to love them.

American author Chanel Miller, victim of sexual-assault perpetrator Brock Turner, wrote in her memoir *Know My Name* that coming out to people she knew about her experience of sexual assault was much harder, because 'they contain pockets of your past, who you were, "you" they believed you to be'. Coming out to someone with your trauma means shattering what they knew of you and mixing in new stuff. That stuff might not be welcome or accurate or fair. And that is the risk, that the trauma will replace the other stuff – the earlier 'you' – and you will be exposed as a fraud of some kind. People I love might feel that they never really knew me. Worst of all, they will be hurt and sad, and people in their lives might judge *them*. But I have to let them know about the parts of me that were not okay, and that maybe are still not okay, and that, in itself, is okay. I cannot protect them or myself from the pain that this will bring them. But when the time comes, I can make space for that chaos, for the grief, for my shaken identity to re-form before their eyes. And maybe it won't be so bad. We really have no idea what is coming. We can assume and speculate and ruminate, but we won't know until it is happening. Our next breath is unknown until we are breathing it.

I am finishing this book in the Tyrone Guthrie Centre in Annaghmakerrig, County Monaghan. I spent the first couple of days reminding myself how lucky I am to be here. I remind myself to make the most of it, to take in the beautiful surroundings, to work hard, to use the time well. I remind myself with every cup of coffee and every conversation and every opening of my laptop, how lucky I am. With every keyboard click: *You're so lucky. Don't forget how lucky you are. This is such a privilege.* I am at the lake, emotionally clinging to the swans floating past, feeling needy, telling myself to remember to be in the moment, to take it in.

I think I'm missing the point.

I had a weird morning, so I went for a drive around the roads, saw a pony in a field and came back. Then I went by the lake, barely visible under a veil of mist. I hung around in the ordinariness of the grass, the ordinariness of the mist, the ordinariness of gravel crunching as someone walked along the path behind me. I realise that although I had been feeling a deep loneliness for many months, I have not felt lonely at all since I arrived here, despite being in a houseful of strangers, despite the minimal human contact. It's just me and my work, which is really saying it's just me.

I'm learning so much about trauma while I'm here, how it moves like seasons within us, how it has its place in the natural order of things. I'm here beside the lake, and I feel an *okayness* within myself. The skin I wear around my body is a comfortable old cardigan. I breathe in and I breathe out, let the lake inhale me into her soft, white cloak. I am just here, a woman. I have nothing to do. I have no tasks, no deadline. When we take away all the distraction of our everyday lives, we are left with our internal stuff, our naturally occurring self. I am just within myself. I sit on the wet grass. I don't need to seek out nature to get something from it. I need to be in nature to help me access connection to the naturally occurring being I am.

We are not separate to nature, occasionally visiting it for walks with the dog, returning to non-natural life afterwards. I am as much the lake as the lake is me. All we are is nature. And so we are faultless, we are above judgement.

I drive home and tell myself, Someday you will feel like a whole person. You won't feel dirty. You will be content to inhabit your body. You will love your body. You won't always be questioning your existence. You won't always hold memories tight in your mind, wound up ready to spring out. Someday the associations will pixellate and fade. Someday you will be able to express yourself and your deepest wants and not feel ashamed. Someday you will be loved again. Someday you might grow a baby inside you and not feel afraid that you will be a terrible mother or a self-absorbed mother or a resentful mother or an overly protective mother. You won't feel that even an unborn baby could reject you because of your past.

Shame will not tighten itself around your throat. You will keep helping people. You are good at it. You will keep writing, and you won't be afraid because you have done *this*, the scariest thing you could ever imagine doing. You will be happy and you will be free. You won't be lonely, or you might, but that will be okay too. You'll collect stones on the beach with your dog. You'll feel more and more part of the natural world. All this will happen. All this is happening. Open your arms at the edge of the sea, and feel the cold air gliding over your skin; open yourself to the world.

I go to the beach and stare at the sea, watch the turnstones running over the seaweed in compact packs. The dog digs holes and whines for attention. My skin has goosebumps and the tips of my fingers are white with cold. My hair is frizzed from the mist, clinging wetly to my neck. We go home, taking the long way round through the village, up the steps, in the door. The dog hops into her bed and I turn on the coffee machine. This is where I'll leave it, allowing myself to stop here, where I am, in early winter, looking out at the drizzle and browning flowers outside my window, and let myself fall softly into the order of things.

ACKNOWLEDGEMENTS

I am grateful to have had the support of so many wonderful people in the creation of this book.

Thank you to my agent Jonathan Williams for his great care and support of me and this book, and for his wisdom and reassurance. Thank you to my publisher Ciara Considine for her immediate belief and trust in the book, her thoughtful editing and gentle way, and to Elaine Egan and Joanna Smyth from Hachette Books Ireland for their passionate commitment and enthusiasm for the book. Thank you to Ami Smithson for the perfect and beautiful cover. Thank you to Edna O'Brien for her encouragement, which I will always remember. Thank you to Brian Langan for his sensitive feedback of the early drafts and consistent encouragement despite my consistently unwavering self-doubt. Thank you to Eoin McHugh for the coffee in 2015. Thank you to Vanessa Fox O'Loughlin for the generosity of a phone call, as I wrestled with deciding what kind of book I was writing. Thank you to the writing teachers I have had over the years for their encouragement and honesty: Mary O'Donnell, Niamh Campbell, Gavin Kostick, and many more.

Thank you to all survivors of sexual violence who have spoken out publicly to make change – your power is immense. Thank you for the generosity of your courage. Thank you to the workers on helplines, in rape crisis centres and domestic abuse refuges, and the court and SATU accompaniers. Thank you to all volunteers. Thank you to feminist campaigners who persist in naming what is right and true despite harassment and hostility. Thank you to Mary Crilly of the Sexual Violence Centre Cork, Noeline Blackwell of the Dublin Rape Crisis Centre, and Tom Clonan, for their work on sexual violence justice. Thank you to all at SPACE International. Thank you to Jackson Katz and Robert Jensen for their work in engaging men. Thank you to those who face into the darkness of male violence against women.

Thank you to the art makers for showing me what beauty is possible when you risk showing yourself to the world. To Grace Dyas for texting me *it's the truth, it's the truth, it's the truth*, when I asked her to remind me why the book is a good idea. To Louise White for her encouragement. To Bryan Borroughs for facilitating more than he could know, and Raymond Keane for inviting me to access the below, below and above, above of myself: Thank you for the 'therapy on speed' that was *I A Clown*. To Mary Coughlan for her music and her courage. To Ste Murray for his gentle way. To the comedian Shane Clifford for making me laugh and reminding me to hold life and myself lightly. Thank you to Dennis Tirch for holding the very special meditative space during the Coronavirus pandemic: it was my valuable reminder that I am love, and that 'there are no others'. To the late Ram Dass for his legacy of compassionate awareness. To my former therapist Caroline for helping me get the words out. Thank you to all psychotherapists for choosing this sometimes lonely but always meaningful work of human connection. Thank you for being the kind of person who wants to help.

Thank you to all at IICP, especially Triona and Pam. Thank you to Judith Herman, Peter Levine, Christiane Sanderson and Rob T. Muller for their contributions to our understanding of trauma. Thank you to the following people for a specific act of support and friendship: Ross Hetherington, Christina Van Der Kamp, Daisy Gaffney, Lauren Larkin and Peter Daly, Sarah Benson and Women's Aid, L.A. Ronayne, Mary Clancy, Sinead Fulcher, Shaun Dunne, Gemma Collins, Fintan Ryan, Phoebe Dick, Claire Twyford, Ruth Breslin and Monica O'Connor, Tom Meagher, Joseph Byrne, Caitlin Roper, Kev Banfield, Damien Quill and Laura Dowling, John-Michael Maher, and Avril Darcy.

Thank you to my yoga teachers, David and Paula, for their wisdom and humour, and for supporting me in deepening into the anchor that is a yoga practice. To my former English teacher Mr. B for allowing me to vent about the impossibilities of writing this book for endless hours in his kitchen, and for all the books. Thank you to Howbert & Mays garden centre for all the plants and plant-based conversations. To my neighbours, the McDonough family, for very often being the best part of the day as I went through this process, especially during the first Covid19 lockdown. To Cafe du Journal for letting me write in a corner with one coffee for five hours. To Claire F for sharing the joy of gardening. To my sister Simona for the fleamarkets, the Apfeltaschen, the calm homecoming that is visiting you in Berlin.

To the men in my life who help heal my heartaches with their heart, courage, love and tenderness: My dad W (I do not have enough words to describe how much I love you), Stephen, Dave and Eric, Ross, Tom, Dave Clown, Fintan, Kev and Damo. Thank you 'C', for being with me every week, from the beginning. Thank you for the miraculous gift – the space, the trust and the respect – and for always being the same. I am so grateful.

I am immensely gifted with friends; thank you for being so solidly there and for bringing me so much joy, especially Tom, Daisy, and Claire T. Thank you to my dear pal Rachel Moran for unwavering presence through all the ups and downs, for the rants and the hilarious times, and Mary – my constant ally in feminism and migraines. Thank you to Riadhna Holohan, without whom this book would not have been written, for radiating love, acceptance and support at each stage of this process and every moment in between. Thank you for listening to me as we traversed Killiney Hill all those times with the dogs.

A very special thank you to 'the girls' for being my reason and my strength for doing this. Thank you for being my people to hang out with on days it was hard to write. Most importantly of all, thank you to my parents, my brilliant mum and dad, for creating the conditions in which I felt safe enough to write this book. Thank you for bearing this exposure of their youngest with such grace and generosity. Thank you for the support and utter acceptance of what I am doing. Finally, thank you to my beloved Jack Russell Terrier, Missy, my tiny companion, who shows me what unconditional love is in every moment, with every glance up, every little stretch, every breath.

FURTHER READING

Judith Lewis Herman, *Trauma and Recovery*

Peter A. Levine, *In an Unspoken Voice*

Peter A. Levine, *Waking the Tiger*

Alice Miller, *The Drama of Being a Child*

Bessel Van Der Kolk, *The Body Keeps the Score*

Irvin Yalom, *Love's Executioner*

Irvin Yalom, *The Gift of Therapy*

Ram Dass & Mirabai Bush, *Walking Each Other Home*

Viktor E. Frankl, *Man's Search for Meaning*

Babette Rothschild, *The Body Remembers*

C.S. Lewis, *A Grief Observed*

Ram Dass, *Paths to God: Living the Bhagavad Gita*

Pema Chödrön, *When Things Fall Apart*

Pema Chödrön, *The Places that Scare You*

Gail Dines, *Pornland*

Robert Jensen, *Getting Off*

Kate Holden, *In My Skin*

Janice Raymond, *Not a Choice, Not a Job*

Julie Bindel, *The Pimping of Prostitution*

Chanel Miller, *Know My Name*

Victor Malarek *The Johns*

Andrea Dworkin, *Letters from a War Zone*

Rachel Moran, *Paid For*

Jackson Katz, *The Macho Paradox*

Pamela Paul, *Pornified*

bell hooks, *All About Love*

Max Porter, *Grief Is The Thing with Feathers*

Heather O'Neill, *Lullabies for Little Criminals*

Kate Elizabeth Russell, *My Dark Vanessa*

Naomi Alderman, *The Power*

Lisa Taddeo, *Three Women*

Jade Sharma, *Problems*

Emilie Pine, *Notes to Self*

Eimear McBride, *A Girl is a Half-formed Thing*

Raven Leilani, *Luster*

Edna O'Brien, *Girl*

Kerrie O'Brien, *Illuminate*

Mary Oliver, *Devotions*